# Where Are They Now?

## CHELSEA F.C.

### Neil Fissler & Andy Pringle

Media House Books

First published in 2010 by
Media House Books
PO Box 466, Eastleigh
Hampshire SO50 0AA

ISBN 978 0 9554937 5 1

Printed and bound in Great Britain by Hobbs the Printers Ltd, Southampton

# Introduction

You may not be surprised to learn that the idea of 'Where Are They Now?' was first discussed in a pub! A pre-match conversation one wet Saturday was triggered by the sight of a couple of former players who hadn't been seen for a few years. We wondered what they had been doing since retiring from the game and the idea for a book was born.

It was a great excuse (and fairly surreal) to meet famous former players and to wallow in nostalgia with the characters who had made growing up as a football fan so exciting.

The first edition was effectively self-published and very quickly became an 'underground' hit. 1,000 copies were printed and sold out almost immediately. Remarkably, it can still be found advertised on Amazon.

Labelled the 'Bog-readers Bible' and the 'Anorak's Almanac', it appeared to capture the imagination and was regularly listed by the Sunday Times as the best selling sports book of the week.

The second edition quickly followed and this also proved to be a major success, again topping the best selling sports book charts.

That was back in 1996, but the thrill of the hunt remained as strong as ever and has prompted us to track down some of the most famous names to have ever worn the Chelsea shirt.

A project like this couldn't have been possible without the help of many people but special thanks must go to Leigh Edwards, who has never grown tired of our phone calls crying "HELP!". Also to Rod George and Dan Davies who supplied many of the superb photos which have helped make this book what it is.

We hope you enjoy the read.

Neil Fissler (London), Andy Pringle (Romsey)

## AGGREY, Jimmy

*(1995-1997)*
Career: *Chelsea, Fulham, Airdrie, Torquay United.* Former trainee who went on to play almost 100 games for Torquay United. Upon retirement from the game, took to acting and played the part of Willam Laurent Dioup in 'Dream Team'.

## ALCIDES

*(2004-2008)*
Career: *Shalke 04, Santos, Chelsea, Benfica (loan), PSV Eindhoven (loan), Dnipr.* Brazilian who won the Portuguese title with Benfica while registered as a Chelsea player. This was one of two loan spells, the other with PSV Eindhoven, that the young defender spent away from the club before signing permanently for Dnipro Dnipropetrovsk in April 2008. An article in the Daily Mail in 2008 quoted that he had been kidnapped but released when his captors were persuaded to believe that he was not a footballer.

## ALEKSIDZE, Rati

*Appearances: 3 Goals: 0 (1999-2002)*
Career: *Chelsea (1999-2002).* Georgian international impressed on trial and was signed permanently for £120,000 from Dynamo Tbilisi. He he never quite fitted into the club's style of play and found himself out in cold after only a handful of appearances. Went back to his former club before retiring for three years. Returned to the game with FC Lokomotivi Tbilisi and has since moved to Hungary to play for Gyorp ETO FC.

Photo: Sicknote 10

## ALLEN, Clive

*Appearances: 16 Goals:7 (1991-1992)*
Career: *Queens Park Rangers, Arsenal, Crystal Palace, Queens Park Rangers, Spurs, Manchester City, Chelsea, West Ham United, Millwall, Carlisle United (1978-1995).* A seasoned striker who followed in the footsteps of his father Les when Ian Porterfield paid £250,000 to bring him to Stamford Bridge in December 1991. This was due to an injury to Kevin Wilson but his stay only four months. Had a spell as a kicker with London Monarchs in NFL Europe and became a successful media pundit. He is now development coach at Spurs.

**GUESS WHO?** - see page 150 for answers.  *Photo: Rod George*

## ALLEN, Les

*Appearances: 49 Goals: 11 (1954-1959)*
*Career: Chelsea, Tottenham Hotspur,*
*Queens Park Rangers. (1956-1968).* Was
an apprentice at Ford's motor plant in
Dagenham when he signed for Chelsea
as an amateur in September 1954. A centre
forward with an eye for goal, he scored 11
goals in 44 appearances for the club but
was struggled to make a first team impact.
Spurs boss Bill Nicholson swapped him for
former England international Johnny
Brooks, in what turned out to be a shrewd
move. Managed QPR, Swindon and in
Greece before going back into the motor
industry. Then worked as a professional
model maker from his home in Hornchurch.
He now splits his time between Essex and
the village of Souni near Limasol in Cyprus.
His sons Clive and Bradley, brother Dennis,
nephews Martin and Paul and Grandson
Oliver have all played professionally.

*JOE ALLON*
*Photo: www.playersincevents.co.uk*

## ALLISTER, Jack

*Appearances: 4 Goals: 1 (1949-1952)*
*Career: Chelsea. Chesterfield. (1949-*
*1958).* A hard working wing half who
could also play at centre forward. Was
basically a reserve during his three year
stay at the club even though he scored the
winner on his debut against Newcastle
United. Worked as a plumber while
playing Highland League football,
coached at Stirling Albion before heading
to Australia. Was unable to secure a
coaching job and therefore returned to
Scotland. Lived in Edinburgh and
continued in the plumbing trade until a
heart attack forced him into an early
retirement. He died in 1999. His daughter
married Ian Porterfield.

## ALLON, Joe

*Appearances: 18 Goals: 3 (1991-1992)*
*Career: Newcastle United, Swansea City,*
*Hartlepool United, Port Vale, Chelsea,*
*Brentford, Port Vale, Lincoln City,*
*Hartlepool United. (1984-1998).*

The Blues paid £250,000 for the Geordie
hit man in August 1991 after finishing the
previous season as top scorer in Division
Four. The dressing room joker never
made an impact at the club and was sold
in December 1992 for £275,000. Since
retiring he has worked on local radio in
the North East and had a spell on the
coaching staff at Leeds United. He is now
a director of a North East based
entertainments company Players Inc.

## AMBROSETTI, Gabrielle

*Appearances: 23 Goals: 1 (1999-2002)*
*Career: Chelsea. (1999-2002).* A £3.5
million signing from Vicenza when
Gianluca Vialli beat off Perugia and Lazio
to sign him. Was dubbed the "Italian Ryan
Giggs" after impressing playing against
the club in the UEFA Cup but sadly his
move to London wasn't to be a success
and he was released in December 2002.
Signed for Piacenza but didn't settle, then
played two seasons at Pro Patria before
dropping off the radar.

## AMBROSIO, Marco

*Appearances: 12 Goals: 0 (2003-2004)*
Career: *Chelsea (2003-2004).* Signed by
Claudio Ranieri on a free transfer to back
up Carlo Cudicini, he found his chances
limited, especially after a nightmare
mistake ridden debut against Notts
County in the League Cup. Injuries
earned him a run in the team, and his
superb display helped the Blues to a 2-1
Champions League quarter final victory
over Arsenal. The arrival of Petr Cech saw
him released. Joined Grasshoppers in
Switzerland before returning to Italy to
play for a series of lower division clubs. Is
currently playing for AC FeralpiSalo.

## ANDERTON, Sylvan

*Appearances: 82 Goals: 2 (1959-1962)*
Career: *Reading, Chelsea, Queens Park
Rangers (1951-1963).* Born in Reading,
Anderton became a product of Ted
Drake's youth policy at Elm Park and it was
the same man who paid £15,000 to take
him to Stamford Bridge, in 1959. Known for
his tough tackling, he spent three seasons
playing for the Blues, before making the
short move across West London to QPR.
Managed Andover, then settled in Bideford,
Devon, where he wrote poetry and scouted
for his home town club Reading.

## ARMSTRONG, Ken

*Appearances: 402 Goals: 30 (1946-1957)*
Career: *Chelsea (1947-1956).* Joined the
club in 1946 from Bradford Rovers for a
fee of 100 guineas, becoming a first team
regular for the next 11 years. He was a
key member of the Blues' 1955
Championship winning team and has
been described as a 'dynamic
orchestrator in the middle of the park'.
Armstrong emigrated to New Zealand in
1957 and continued to play until he was
almost 47. Already capped once by
England in 1955, he went onto to
represent New Zealand nine times scoring
three goals. Became national coach of
New Zealand between 1958 and 1964.
Died in 1984 and his ashes were then
strewn over the pitch at Stamford Bridge.

## ATHERTON, Robert

*Appearances: 0 Goals: (1906)*
Career: *Middlesbrough, Chelsea. (1903-
1906).* Moved to Scotland as a youngster
but played for Wales. Was captain of
Middlesbrough when he moved to
Stamford Bridge but never played a first
team game after aggravated an injury he
suffered the previous season. Worked as a
commercial traveller for a firm of office
suppliers but was killed during WW1
when the submarine he was serving on
was lost at sea.

Photo: Rod George

## AYLOTT, Trevor

*Appearances: 32 Goals: 2 (1975-1979)*
Career: *Chelsea, Barnsley, Millwall, Luton
Town, Crystal Palace, Barnsley,
Birmingham City, Oxford United,
Gillingham, Wycombe Wanderers, (1976-
1993.)* Was a teenager from Bermondsey
when given the chance to shine. He
responded by scoring the winning goals
in his first two games, against Bristol City
and Notts Forest, both ironically in the 55th
minute. Sadly, it only proved to be a short
term fix and he failed to find the net again.
Was shipped off to Barnsley in 1979 for
the first of many transfers. He has driven a
London Black Cab since hanging up his
boots and has also worked for the Press
Association.

Photo: Michael Kjaer

# BABAYARO, Celestin

*Appearances: 197 Goals: 8 (1997-2005)*
Career: *Chelsea, Newcastle United (1997-2008)*. Aged only18, he was the most expensive teenager in the club history when he cost £2.25 million from Belgian outfit Anderlecht in April 1997. He was already an established international with an Olympic Gold medal and won over the Stamford Bridge faithful when he made his debut against Leicester City. He faced competition from Graeme Le Saux and then Wayne Bridge during his time at the club but was part of the 2000 FA Cup winning side. Only played four games in the 2004/05 title win and left to join Newcastle United in January 2005. He now owns a sheep farm in France and is also believed to be doing corporate work in his native Nigeria.

# BAKER, Ben-Howard

*Appearances: 93 Goals: 1 (1921-1926)*
Career: *Preston North End, Liverpool, Everton, Chelsea, Oldham Athletic, Everton. (1915-1929)*.

An amateur throughout his football career, Baker represented Great Britain in the Triple Jump and High Jump at the 1912 and 1920 Olympic Games. He won six AAA titles in the High Jump and held the British record. Is still the only goalkeeper to have scored for the club, his goal coming against Bradford City in 1921. Joined the family firm of soap and chemical manufacturers and became a prominent businessman in the Liverpool area. died in Warminster in September 1997 aged 95.

# BALDWIN, Pat

*(2001-2002)*
Career: *Chelsea, Colchester United, Bristol Rovers (loan), Southend United (loan)*. Centre back who was a junior at Stamford Bridge before moving to Colchester United in 2002. Became a fans' favourite and won all four of the Club's Player of the Year awards in 2004-5. Loaned to Southend United in January 2010.

# BALDWIN, Tommy

*Appearances 239 Goals: 92 (1966-1974)*
Career: *Arsenal, Chelsea, Millwall, Manchester United, Brentford. (1964-1977)*. Known as the 'Sponge' for his ability to absorb alcohol. Arrived at Stamford Bridge in a swap deal for George Graham and made an immediate impact scoring the first of 17 goals in his first season on his debut against Manchester City in October 1966. He was part of the Blues' first ever FA Cup Final success against Leeds United in 1970 and then was in the team that recorded the Cup Winners Cup Final victory over Real Madrid. After this, he was unable to hold down a regular first team place. As a result, in September 1975, was deemed surplus to requirements by Dave Sexton and handed a free transfer. He now lives just down the road in Fulham and has worked in property development and the media.

Photo: SpreePix

## BALLACK, Michael

*Appearances: 105  Goals: 17 (2006-2010)*
*Career: Chemnitz, Kaiserslauten, Bayer Leverkusen, Bayern Munich, Chelsea, Bayer Leverkusen (1995-2010).* Re-joined one of his former clubs, Bayer Leverkusen on a free transfer in June 2010.

## BAMBRICK, Joe

*Appearances: 66  Goals: 37 (1934-1938)*
*Career: Chelsea, Walsall (1934-1939).*
The only player in international football history to score six goals in a game for Northern Ireland. Four years after achieving the feat, Chelsea beat off competition from a whole host of other clubs to pay Linfield what was then a huge transfer fee of £2,500. During his four years at the club he was leading scorer for two seasons and his most memorable performance was netting four times in the 7-1 victory of Leeds in 1935. He moved to Walsall in 1938 and then returned to Belfast after the outbreak of WW2. Bambrick continued to serve Linfield as coach and scout for many years. He died on 13 October 1983, aged 79 and a blue plaque can be seen on the front of his former home at 219 Roden Street, Belfast.

## BANNON, Eamonn

*Appearances: 27  Goals: 1 (1979)*
*Career: Chelsea 1979.* Bought for £200,000 by Danny Blanchflower to replace Steve Wicks and Kenny Swain in a bid to turn around a desperate season. When the Irish manager was sacked and replaced by Geoff Hurst, it wasn't long before Bannon slipped down the pecking order and later that year he was sold to Dundee United for a then Scottish record fee of £165,000. He went on to manage Falkirk but after suing them for breach of contract he bought the Strathallan Guest House in his home city of Edinburgh with the proceeds. He also does matchday work for the Press Association.

## BARKAS, Ned

*Appearances: 28  Goals: 0 (1937-1939)*
*Career: Norwich City, Huddersfield Town, Bimingham City, Chelsea (1920-1939).*
Was past his best when he arrived at Stamford Bridge to be reunited with his previous manager Leslie Knighton. A former miner was working as a storeman in Little Bromwich, Birmingham at the time of his death aged 61 in April 1962.

## BARNARD, Darren

*Appearances: 33  Goals: 2 (1990-1995)*
*Career: Chelsea, Reading, Bristol City, Barnsley, Grimsby Town, Aldershot Town (1990-2007).* Darren was a surprise £100,000 signing from non league Wokingham Town as an 18 year-old but he had to wait two years to make his league debut because of the Gareth Hall and Frank Sinclair pairing. It wasn't until the caretaker management of David Webb that he was given a regular run. He played in the FA Cup semi final win over Luton Town but failed to convince Glenn Hoddle that he had a long term future and he was sold to Bristol City for £750,000 after 18 months out of the team. The former Welsh international is now General Manager of Camberley Town having joined them as Director of Football in 2007.

**GUESS WHO? - see page 150 for answers.** *Photo: Dan Davies*

## BARNESS, Anthony

*Appearances: 19 Goals: 0 (1992-1996)*
Career: *Charlton Athletic, Chelsea, Middlesbrough, Southend United, Charlton Athletic, Bolton Wanderers, Plymouth Argyle (1991-2007).* It is said that the Blues only signed Barness for £350,000 because they failed to land his Charlton team mate Scott Minto. During his four years at the club he couldn't establish himself and he was loaned out twice before returning to The Valley for £165,000. He has been playing for non league Lewes since 2007.

## BARRACLOUGH, Bill

*Appearances: 81 Goals: 11 (1934-1937)*
Career: *Hull City, Wolverhampton Wanderers, Chelsea. (1928-1937).* A winger who was a regular in the Chelsea team for two and a half seasons but was said to have become a target of the boo-boys of the time. He returned to his native Hull, worked as a clerk in the docks and later became a fruit merchant. Died in August 1969 aged 60

## BARRETT, Neil

*(2001-2004)*
Career: *Chelsea, Portsmouth, Dundee, Livingston, Woking, Ebbsfleet United, York City (2001-date).* Former junior, now playing for York City.

## BARRON, Jim

*Appearances: 1 Goals: 0 (1965-1966)*
Career: *Wolves, Chelsea, Oxford United, Nottingham Forest, Swindon Town, Peterborough United. (1961-1981).* Signed for £5,000 from Wolves in April 1965 to be understudy to Peter Bonetti. Only made one appearance for Chelsea and he left for Oxford United towards the end of the same season. He has since managed Cheltenham Town and been caretaker boss of Northampton, where he is currently first team coach. Ran his own goalkeeping school in Gloucestershire, was on the Crystal Palace coaching staff and served a short prison sentence for a road crash that killed his wife.

## BASON, Brian

*Appearances: 22 Goals: 1 (1972-1977)*
Career: *Chelsea, Plymouth Argyle, Crystal Palace, Portsmouth, Reading. (1972-1982).* Brian made his first team debut in 1972 soon after his 17th birthday but struggled to hold down a regular first team place. In 1976, just as it looked like he was making some headway, a clash with Sammy Nelson left him with a double fracture of the right shin. Within 18 months he was sold to Plymouth for £30,000. Managed an hotel in Truro, Cornwall after hanging up his boots, then ran several pubs in the Home Counties before moving to Daventry to work as a sales rep.

## BATHGATE, Sid

*Appearances: 147 Goals: 0 (1946-1953)*
Career: *Chelsea (1946-1952)*. Full back, who served in the RAF during World War 2, and was signed by Chelsea after his demob. Made his debut against Liverpool in January 1947 and became a regular in the team before moving to Scotland. He was married three sons and two daughters and died in 1963 aged 43.

## BEASANT, Dave

*Appearances: 157 Goals: 0 (1989-1993)*
Career: *Wimbledon, Newcastle United, Chelsea, Grimsby Town, Wolves, Southampton, Nottingham Forest, Portsmouth, Spurs, Bradford City, Wigan, Brighton, Fulham. (1979-2004)*. Cost the Blues a club record £725,000 and went onto became part of the Second Division Championship and ZDS winning teams. Came under pressure from Kevin Hitchcock in the early 90's after a string of injuries. Ian Porterfield made it clear he had no future at the club after he gifted Norwich victory in September 1992.

When David Webb took over, he was recalled but never looked at ease and was eventually replaced by Dmitri Kharine. Following his retirement in 2004, Beasant went on to become a goalkeeping coach firstly for the Northern Ireland side, and then for Fulham. In 2008, he began working in the Glenn Hoddle Academy School as a senior coach.

## BECKFORD, Jermaine

*(2000-2003)*
Career: *Chelsea, Wealdstone, Leeds United, Everton (2000-date)*. Ealing born former youth team player who, having failed to win a pro contract, joined Wealdstone in the Isthmian League and scored 54 goals in only 82 games. He was also working as windscreen fitter for the RAC until Leeds United beat off a host of interested clubs to sign him up in 2006. Signed for Everton in August 2010.

## BELL, Dr John

*Appearances: 44 Goals: 10 (1920-1923)*
Career: *Chelsea. (1920-1923)*. Bell was said to be the fastest winger in Scotland when he arrived from Queens Park but never found his best form for the club and wasn't considered to be a fans' favourite. He returned to Scotland to join Hamilton, continued to practice as a doctor, died in Scotland in 1980 aged 79.

## BELLETT, Wally

*Appearances: 35 Goals: 1 (1954-1958)*
Career: *Chelsea, Plymouth Argyle, Leyton Orient, Chester City, Wrexham, Tranmere Rovers. (1954-1964)*. Joined the Blues in September 1954 after an impressive trial from Barking Town. He had to wait 18 months for his league debut but never became a regular and was sold to Plymouth in a double deal with Len Casey. Moved to Essex when his career ended and coached Canvey Island for many years while working as a lorry driver and car mechanic. Now lives in retirement.

## BELLETTI, Juliano

*Appearances: 94 Goals: 5 (2007-2010)
Career: Cruzeiro, Sao Paulo, Atletico
Mineiro (loan), Villareal, Barcelona,
Chelsea, Fluminese (1994-2010).* Brazilian
right back was released at the end of his
two year contract and signed for
Fluminese in his home-land in July 2010.

## BEN HAIM, Tel

*Appearances: 13 Goals: 0 (2007-2008)
Career: Maccabi Tel Aviv, Bolton
Wanderers, Chelsea, Manchester City,
Sunderland (loan), Portsmouth, West Ham
United (2001-2010).* Followed ex-Chelsea
and Portsmouth manager Avram Grant
from Pompey to West Ham before the start
of the 2010-2011 season.

*Photo: www.sport-memorabilia.co.uk*

## BENTLEY, Roy

*Appearances: 367 Goals: 150 (1948-1956)
Career: Bristol City, Newcastle United,
Chelsea, Fulham, Queens Park Rangers
(1939-1962).* Signed for Chelsea for
£12,500 because a doctor advised him a
move south would help a lung problem.
Ironically, it was the same reason that
persuaded the man he was replacing,
Tommy Lawton, to join the club as well.
Bentley struggled to adapt to the Blues'
style of play, but as soon as he did he

ended his first season at the club as
leading scorer with 23 goals. This was was
something that he did for each of his eight
seasons at Stamford Bridge. The highlight
of his time at the club was skippering
them to their 1954-55 League
Championship success. Went onto
become one of the first members of the
aging squad to be sold. Managed both
Reading and Swansea, and returned to the
Royals as secretary in 1977. Then moved
onto Aldershot, ended his working life
filling a similar role at a golf club and a
lake fishing business, both run by Ron
Harris, now lives in retirement in Reading.

## BERRY, Paul

*Appearances: 3 Goals: 0 (1953-1960)
Career: Chelsea (1953-1960).* Spent most
of his seven years at the club in the
second and third string but made his first
team debut against Manchester City in
March 1957. Berry only went onto to play
two more games before he was released
and joined Tonbridge. He lived Grays,
Essex until his death in a car accident in
2000.

## BETTRIDGE, Walter

*Appearances: 255 Goals: 0 (1909-1922)
Career: Chelsea, Gillingham (1909-1923).*
An FA Cup runner up in 1915, after
keeping Jack Harrow out of the team and
was a regular for almost the whole of his
nine years at the club. An attacking full
back, his partner was Jock Cameron in the
1912 promotion winning side. Was mine
host at Bird-in-Hand in Measham, Leics,
when he died in December 1931 aged 43.

## BILLINGTON, Hugh

*Appearances: 83 Goals: 28 (1951-1952)
Career: Luton Town, Chelsea, Worcester
City (1937-1952).* Prolific goal-scorer
whose career was interrupted by the
Second World War. Joined Chelsea in
1948 for £8,000 from Luton Town, where
he had scored 63 goals in 87 games. Died
in the Luton area in 1988.

*Photo: Antonia Sterland*

## BIRCHENALL, Alan, MBE

*Appearances: 96  Goals: 28 (1967-1970)*
*Career: Sheffield United, Chelsea, Crystal Palace, Leicester City, Notts County, Blackburn Rovers, Luton Town, Hereford United. (1964-1979).* One of the first players to be transferred for a six figure fee when he joined The Blues for £100,000. He appeared to be set for a long career at the club but suffered a knee injury in a clash with WBA keeper Ian McFaul. During the three months he was was out of action, Ian Hutchinson and Peter Osgood struck up their legendary double act and the arrival of Keith Weller effectively ended his stint at the Bridge. The Blues got their money back by selling him to Crystal Palace. He later joined Leicester's public relations department, where he can still be found as a half time host. Alan's commercial interests have included owning a village pub and running a ladies footwear import business.

## BIRNIE, Ted

*Appearances: 101  Goals: 3 (1906-1909)*
*Career: Newcastle United, Crystal Palace, Chelsea, Tottenham Hotspur.* After a successful playing career as a wing half, Birnie became one of the first Englishmen to coach a German side (FC Mulheim). He later managed Southend United for over 500 games. Died in 1935 aged 55.

## BISHOP, Syd

*Appearances: 109  Goals: 6 (1928-1933)*
*Career: West Ham United, Leicester City, Chelsea. (1920-1933).* Played in the first ever Wembley Cup Final. Joined Chelsea for £3,800 and two years later was part of the team which won promotion to the First Division in 1930. Within three years he had retired through injury. Died suddenly at his Chelsea home in 1949 aged 49.

## BLAKE, Nathan

*Career: Cardiff City, Sheffield United, Bolton Wanderers, Blackburn Rovers, Wolverhampton Wanderers, Leicester City, Leeds United (loan), Newport County (1990-2006).* Despite being released from the youth set-up in 1990, Blake carved out a successful career in the lower divisions and earned 29 caps for his country (Wales). He left the game in 2006 to spend more time running his property management company in Wales.

## BLOCK, Micky

*Appearances: 40  Goals: 6 (1957-1962)*
*Career: Chelsea, Brentford, Watford. (1957-1967).* A product of the clubs flourishing nursery and member of the Blues' 1957-58 FA Youth Cup Final team. Made his debut aged 17 but within two years, the first team dressing room door was slammed shut as he fell behind Peter Brabrook and Frank Blunstone in the pecking order. Is still a regular visitor to Stamford Bridge, living in North London and works as a black cab driver.

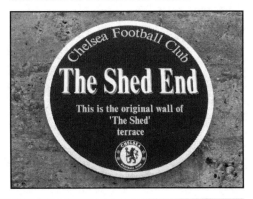

**Peter Bonetti.** *Courtesy of www.sport-memorabilia.co.uk*

## BLUNSTONE, Frank

*Appearances: 347 Goals: 54 (1953-1964)*
Career: *Crewe Alexandra, Chelsea. (1951-1964)*. Was an important part of the 1954-55 Championship winning side and a key player during the whole of his Stamford Bridge career. Lost pace because of a broken leg and a second broken leg ended his career. Went onto become the Chelsea youth team coach, had two spells as Brentford manager and assistant manager, youth and reserve team coach at Manchester United. Now lives in retirement in his native Crewe.

## BODLEY, Mickey

*Appearances: 8 Goals: 1 (1985-1989)*
Career: *Chelsea, Northampton Town, Barnet, Southend United, Gillingham, Birmingham City, Peterborough United. (1985-1999)*. Came through the ranks and made his debut against Norwich in 1987. Failed to hold down a regular place and was sold to Northampton for £50,000. Now works as a postman in Essex.

## BOGARDE, Winston

*Appearances: 12 Goals: 0 (2000-2004)*
Career: *Chelsea (2001-2004)*. Only made 12 appearances in four seasons, despite having a CV that reads like a who's who of club football. Gianluca Vialli claimed the signing was nothing to do with him and was conducted by Colin Hutchinson. As soon as Claudio Ranieri took over, Bogarde was sent training with the youth team in a bid to get him to leave the club, but he was happy on £40,000 a week wages and openly admitted it: "This world is about money, so when you are offered those millions you take them. Few people will ever earn so much. I am one of the few fortunates who do. I may be one of the worst buys in the history of the Premiership, but I don't care." He retired after leaving Stamford Bridge. Was working in the entertainment industry but is now studying for diploma Pro Coach Football in Belfast, Northern Ireland.

## BOLLAND, Gordon

*Appearances: 2 Goals: 0 (1960-1962)*
Career: *Chelsea, Leyton Orient, Norwich City, Charlton Athletic, Millwall (1961-1974)*. Won the FA Youth Cup with The Blues in 1960 and 1961, but only made two first team appearances before being released. Gordon returned to his roots, to live in Boston and to work as a Sales Rep for a tyre company.

## BONETTI, Peter

*Appearances: 729 Goals: 0 (1959-1979)*
Career: *Chelsea (1959-1978)*. Nicknamed 'The Cat', Peter was the son of a Swiss born restaurateur. He was signed by Ted Drake from Reading youths after his mum wrote to the club asking for him to be given a trial. Then spent almost all of the the next 19 seasons as first choice keeper. Played vital roles in League Cup, FA Cup and Cup Winners Cup successes. Only Ron Harris had played more games for the club. He took his family off to the Isle of Mull, where he worked as a postman and occasionally turned out for Scottish league sides. Now lives in Birmingham and has coached goalies for several league clubs as well as helping out with the England squad. Has been involved with the Blues in corporate hospitality and is an in-demand after dinner speaker.

## BOROTA, Petar

*Appearances: 114 Goals: 0 (1979-1982)*
Career: *Chelsea, Brentford (1978-1982)..*
Joined Chelsea from Partizan Belgrade in March 1979 for £70,000 but couldn't prevent the side from slipping to relegation. Kept the first of 36 clean sheets against Liverpool on his League debut and became a cult hero. Was voted Player of the Year in 1981 but was allowed to join Brentford twelve months later after a fall out with John Neal. Returned to Yugoslavia where he ran a Duty Free shop and was then involved in a stolen picture racket resulting in a major court case. He died on 12th February 2010 in Genoa, Italy.

## BOSNICH, Mark

*Appearances: 7 Goals: 0 (2001-2003)*
*Career: Manchester United, Aston Villa,*
*Manchester United, Chelsea (1989-2003).*
Joined the Blues on a free transfer but
injuries delayed his League debut until
later in 2001 because of injury and fitness
problems. He kept a clean sheet against
Leeds on his debut and played the next
five games, but after he went off in the
goal-less draw with Everton, his
replacement, Carlo Cudicini, became first
choice. His football career hit rock bottom
in September 2002 when he failed a
drugs test and was banned for nine
months. Now plays for Australian non-
league side Sydney Olympic. Also a co-
commentator and football pundit on
Australian television and a players agent.

**Khalid Boulahrouz at the 2010 World Cup**
*Photo: sbstheworldgame*

## BOULAHROUZ, Khalid

*Appearances: 13 Goals: 0 (2006-2008)*
*Career: RKSC Waalwijk, Hamburg,*
*Chelsea, Sevilla (loan), Stuttgart (2001-*
*2010).* Dutch international who now plays
in Germany for VfB Stuttgart. He joined
them in July 2008 for a fee believed to be
in the region of £4million. Represented
his country in the 2010 World Cup.

## BOWER, AG

*Appearances: 9 Goals: 0 (1923-1925)*
*Career: Chelsea (1923-1925).* Joined the
London Stock Exchange at the end of the
First World War and remains the only
person to play in the First Division and
work there at the same time. He was
unable to stop the Blues dropping into the
second division but continued to work in
the City until 1954. He then became a
Welfare Officer in Croydon until retiring in
1960. Died in June 1970. Was also a
member of the FA Council

*Photo: CamW*

## BOWIE, Jimmy

*Appearances: 84  Goals: 22 (1944-1951)*
*Career: Chelsea, Fulham, Brentford,*
*Watford, Fulham (1944-1957)*. Cost £25
and played in the War Time Cup Final
defeat to Charlton. Stayed at the club for
seven years before he was sent to Fulham
in exchange for Wally Hinshelwood.
Became a publican in Trowbridge and
then Great Wakering, Essex. Died in
nearby Shoeburyness in August 2000.

## BOWMAN, Andy

*Appearances: 1  Goals: 0 (1951-1955)*
*Career: Chelsea, Newport County (1951-*
*1963)*. A Scottish schoolboy international
who was signed on his 17th birthday and
played his only game in the 1955 title
winning team. Went onto work for Scottish
& Newcastle breweries. Died of a heart
attack in March 2009 aged 74 in Dundee
after suffering from Alzheimer's disease.

## BOYD, Tom

*Appearances 32  Goals: 0 (1991-1992)*
*Career: Chelsea (1991-1992)*. Was signed
from Motherwell for £800,000 to replace
Tony Dorigo, but didn't have the same
attacking flair, and after less than a season
at Stamford Bridge he was swapped with
Celtic's Tony Cascarino. He remains at
Celtic Park as a youth team coach.

## BOYLE, John

*Appearances: 226  Goals: 12 (1964-1973)*
*Career: Chelsea, Brighton & Hove Albion,*
*Leyton Orient (1964-1975)*. Signed for the
Blues while on holiday in London. Scored
the winning goal in the first leg of the
League Cup semi final against Aston Villa
in 1965 on his debut. Picked up a winner's
medal after helping the club to beat
Leicester in the final. Just as it appeared
he was set to take John Hollins' place, he
suffered head injuries in a car accident.
Boyle missed the 1970 FA Cup Final
through injury but returned to the team for
the Cup Winners' Cup final 12 months later.

Was sold to Orient for a small fee. Later
worked as a Security officer in Central
London whilst living in Kent.

## BRABROOK, Peter

*Appearances: 271  Goals: 57 (1955-1962)*
*Career: Chelsea, West Ham United,*
*Leyton Orient (1954-1970)*. Peter made
three appearances as the Blues clinched
the 1955 League title as a 17 year-old and
he became the first Chelsea junior to play
for England. Not all of Drake's Ducklings
made the grade, but he continued play
regularly until Tommy Docherty replaced
Drake as manager. Among the wholesale
changes, Brabrook was sold to West Ham
for £35,000. Ran a butcher's shop, and
worked for a paper tycoon. Later worked
for the West Ham Academy with Frank
Lampard and Joe Cole to name but a few.

## BRADBURY, Terry

*Appearances: 29  Goals: 1 (1957-1962)*
*Career: Chelsea, Southend United, Leyton*
*Orient, Wrexham, Chester City. (1957-*
*1961)*. An aggressive wing half, who had
to wait a long time for his first team
chance. Played within his limitations but
despite a couple of runs in the team
couldn't nail down a regular place and
was part of Tommy Docherty's clear out.
Had a brief spell as Northwich Victoria
boss but settled in Derbyshire, working in
the licensing trade for many years.

## BRADSHAW, Joe

*Appearances: 6  Goals: 3 (1909-1910)*
*Career: Southampton, Arsenal, Fulham,*
*Chelsea, QPR, Southend United. (1900-*
*1913)*. Arrived un-noticed in May 1909
and scored in his first three matches. But
after failing to score in his next three
games, he mysteriously never played for
the club again. Became player manager of
Southend before the Great War, then
afterwards, managed Swansea for seven
seasons, then Fulham and Bristol City
before spending 15 years in the insurance
industry. Died in 1950.

## BRAWN, Billy

*Appearances: 99 Goals: 11 (1907-1911)*
Career: *Northampton Town, Sheffield
United, Aston Villa, Middlesbrough,
Chelsea, Brentford. (1895-1919).* An
England international, Brawn was known
for being one of the best outside rights
around the turn of the last century. With
great speed and accurate shooting, he
enjoyed three good seasons in SW6.
Starred in the clubs first ever season in the
top flight. Was employed at Brentford in a
management advisory capacity and
became a director of the club. Ran a pub
locally until his death in 1932 aged 54.

## BREBNER, Ronald

*Appearances: 19 Goals: 0 (1906-1913)*
Career: *Sunderland, Chelsea, Darlington,
Huddersfield Town, Chelsea, Leicester
Fosse (1905-1914).* Made his Chelsea
debut as a stand-in for Dick Whiting, then
started 17 of 22 games at the start of the
1912-1913 season. A dentist by profession,
he ran his own practice in the North of
England until his death in November 1914
after failed to recover from a bang on the
head he suffered on Boxing Day 1913.

## BRIDGE, Wayne

*Appearances: 87 Goals: 1 (2003-2009)*
Career: *Southampton, Chelsea, Fulham
(loan), Manchester City (1998-2010).*
Joined Manchester City on 2nd January
2009 for a fee in the region of £10 million.

## BRIDGES, Barry

*Appearances: 205 Goals: 93 (1958-1966)*
Career: *Chelsea, Birmingham, Queens
Park Rangers, Millwall, Brighton (1958-
1973).* A schools' sprint champion who
was the complete striker and a key player
for the club during the Docherty era.
Dropped to allow a young Peter Osgood
to play regularly but was reinstated
following a fans' petition. His Stamford
Bridge career came to end a year later
however when he was sent home from the
airport prior to the first leg of a Fairs Cup
tie with Barcelona. After hanging up his
boots, Barry ran a hotel on the Sussex
coast before taking over the running of his
grandfather's farm and starting a milk
round in his native Norfolk. He sold both
businesses to buy a paper shop in West
Earlham. Now semi retired, living in
Taverham providing respite care for
children with special needs.

**Barry Bridges & Bobby Tambling**
*Photo: John Dobson*

## BRILEY, Les
*(1974-1976)*
Career: *Chelsea, Hereford, Wimbledon, Aldershot, Millwall, Brighton (1974-1994).* Started his career at Stamford Bridge but left without ever playing a first team game. Carved out a League career that lasted almost 20 years. Went on to work in the building business. He is now Assistant Youth Academy Manager at Millwall.

## BRITTAN, Harold
*Appearances: 24  Goals: 7 (1913-1920)*
Career: *Chelsea, Leicester Fosse (loan), (1913-1928).* Brittan's brief Chelsea career was broken into two spells by the First World War and was ended by his decision to emigrate to the United States. Once across the water he became a legend before retiring to concentrate on his business interests. His contribution to the sport was recognised with induction into the National Hall of Fame in 1951. He died on 9th April 1964 at the age of 69.

*Photo: Rod George*

## BRITTON, Ian
*Appearances: 289  Goals: 34 (1971-1982)*
Career: *Chelsea, Blackpool, Burnley. (1972-1989).* Signed from Scottish junior side Hillside Rangers in 1972 but it wasn't until the club were relegated three years later and more established players left that he became a regular. Enjoyed another promotion and suffered a second relegation before slipping out of favour

and returning to his native Dundee. He has worked in Leisure Management and writes a column for a local paper in Lancashire.

## BROLLY, Mike
*Appearances: 9  Goals: 1 (1971-1974)*
Career: *Chelsea, Bristol City, Grimsby Town, Derby County, Scunthorpe, Scarborough. (1971-1985).* An old fashioned winger, came through the ranks at Stamford Bridge, but was allowed to leave on a free transfer because he was behind the likes of Charlie Cooke, John Hollins and Alan Hudson. Scored his only goal against Southampton in April 1973. He now lives in the Grimsby area and is an assistant head teacher (his wife is head) of St Mary's RC High School. Also coaches within the District Schools set up.

## BROOKS, Johnny
*Appearances: 52  Goals: 7 (1959-1961)*
Career: *Reading, Tottenham Hotspur, Chelsea, Brentford, Crystal Palace. (1949-1964).* A strong, well built inside forward he was brought to the club from Spurs by Ted Drake, for £20,000 plus Les Allen in December 1959, but like the team he was came into he struggled and despite keeping faith with him for a Drake eventually sold him to Brentford. After football, worked a brokers messenger in the City and now lives in retirement in Kent. His son Shaun played for Leyton Orient and Crystal Palace.

## BROWN, Dennis
*Appearances: 13  Goals: 2 (1962-1964)*
Career: *Chelsea, Swindon Town, Northampton Town, Aldershot (1963-1975).* Started his Blues career as a junior, but was never able to establish himself because of Bobby Tambling and George Graham and was sold to Aldershot for £17,000. Now lives in Wokingham, Berkshire and works as a self employed salesman in the Berkshire and Hampshire area.

## BROWN, William

*Appearances: 57 Goals: 21 (1924-1929)*
*Career: West Ham United, Chelsea,*
*Stockport County, Hartlepool United*
*(1921-1931).* Played for West Ham in the
first ever Wembley Cup Final. Signed in an
unsuccessful attempt to stave off
relegation from the First Division. Scored
on his league debut against WBA, and
despite an impressive scoring record could
never hold down a regular first team place
before leaving for Fulham. Returned to his
native North East where he worked as a
Baths' Superintendent at Easington Colliery,
County Durham. He stood as an umpire for
many years and stayed in the town until his
death in January 1985 aged 85.

## BUCHANAN, Peter

*Appearances: 39 Goals: 6 (1935-1946)*
*Career: Chelsea, Fulham, Brentford*
*(1935-1949).* Winger who played for the
Blues either side of WW2. Died in 1977
aged 61.

## BUMSTEAD, John

*Appearances: 409 Goals: 44 (1976-1991)*
*Career: Chelsea, Charlton Athletic (1978-*
*1993).* Spent a total of 19 years at
Stamford Bridge as schoolboy, trainee and
professional.

**John Bumstead**
*Photo: Rod George*

Went on to do a solid job for a whole
succession of managers who occupied
the hot seat. A free kick specialist, he
played a part in two Division Two
Championship winning and two Full
Members Cup winning teams. His
committed style saw him pick up regular
injuries but he still managed to play over
400 games for the club before joining
Charlton Athletic on a free transfer. He has
coached at Charlton's academy, acted as a
matchday host at The Valley and earns a
crust by driving a black cab.

## BURGESS, Harry

*Appearances: 155 Goals: 37 (1935-1945)*
*Career: Stockport County, Sheffield*
*Wednesday, Chelsea (1926-1945).* Was
recommended to Chelsea by his former
Sheffield Wednesday boss Bob Brown who
was working as a scout, and cost £4,000.
Served the club well in the years leading
up to the World War Two. Joined the police
force during the war, before becoming a
clerk of works for the MoD. Burgess
moved back to Cheshire to run a pub but
was working as a foreman joiner at the
time of his death aged 53 in 1957.

## BURLEY, Craig

*Appearances: 137 Goals: 11 (1989-1997)*
*Career: Chelsea, Derby County, Preston*
*North End, Walsall. (1989-2006).* The
nephew of former Scotland boss George,
wasn't seen as a key player for long
periods of his Stamford Bridge career.
Burley enjoyed his best spells under
Glenn Hoddle and Ruud Gullit, winning
his first medal in the 1997 FA Cup Final
win over Middlesbrough. He never really
settled after leaving the club, despite
spells with Derby County, Preston North
End and Walsall. Opened a restaurant
called the Sanctuary which fell victim to
the recession and went bust in 2008. The
former Scottish international then
accepted the offer to become a pundit on
television firstly for Setanta and now with
ESPN.

**GUESS WHO? - see page 150 for answers.** *Photo: Dan Davies*

## BUTLER, Dennis

*Appearances 18  Goals: 0 (1960-1963)*
*Career: Chelsea, Hull City, Reading*
*(1960-1974).* A member of the Blues' FA
Youth Cup winning sides in 1960 and
1961. However, with Ken Shellito and
Eddie McCreadie ahead of him in the
pecking order, he was sold to Hull City for
£10,000 after only 18 appearances. Ended
his professional career with Reading
before working as a painter and decorator
in the area. Later worked for Rentokil in
London. Has now retired to Bournemouth.

## BUTLER, Geoff

*Appearances: 9  Goals: 0 (1967-1968)*
*Career: Middlesbrough, Chelsea,*
*Sunderland, Norwich City, Bournemouth,*
*Peterborough United. (1965-1981).* Cost
£57,000 but never settled at Stamford
Bridge and was sold after just four months
for an £8,000 profit. Was manager, head of
commercial department and then director
at Salisbury City for 18 years. Now lives in
Shrewton, Wiltshire and has set up his own
home improvement company.

## CALDERHEAD Jnr, David

*Appearances: 43  Goals: 1 (1907-1914)*
*Career: Lincoln City, Chelsea, Clapton*
*Orient. (1906-1921).* Was a regular in the
first team before the outbreak of the First
World War checked his career like so
many others. The son of the former
Chelsea boss by the same name, became
manager of Lincoln City for three years
and owned the Newmarket Hotel in the
same city.

## CAMPBELL, Bobby

*Appearances: 213  Goals: 40 (1947-1954)*
*Career: Chelsea, Reading (1947-1961).*
Cost the club £9,000 after the war, and
proved to be a good investment. Playing
anywhere across the front line, he
probably saw his best years in the game
cut short by the war, but still managed to
win the last of his international caps

playing for Chelsea in 1950. Served
Bristol Rovers as coach, trainer, chief scout
(twice) and managed the first team for 15
years. was also manager at Gloucester
City and worked for Bristol City Council
as a football coach for unemployed men.
Now lives in retirement in Almondsbury

Photo: Rod George

## CANOVILLE, Paul

*Appearances: 103  Goals: 15 (1981-1986)*
*Career: Chelsea, Reading (1981-1987).*
Joined from non league Hillingdon
Borough and became the first black
player in club history when he made his
league debut as a substitute against
Crystal Palace in April 1982 Survived the
gauntlet of racial abuse to help the club to
the Second Division title in 1984, but
within two years was sold to Reading for
£50,000. Since retiring at the age of 24
through injury he has survived cancer and
drug addiction, became a teaching
assistant at a school in Westminster,
worked on the Blues education
programme and set up a company called
Senkaa which starts up youth projects.

## CARVALHO, Ricardo

*Appearances: 135 Goals: 7 (2004-2010)*
*Career: Porto, Leca (loan), Vitoria de*
*Setubal (loan), Alverca (loan), Chelsea,*
*Real Madrid (1997-2010.* Portuguese
international centre back signed for Real
Madrid on 10th August 2010 for a fee of
about £8 million.

## CASCARINO, Tony

*Appearances: 45 Goals: 8 (1992-1994)*
*Career: Gillingham, Millwall, Aston Villa,*
*Chelsea (1981-1994).* A powerful,
aggressive striker who join The Blues for
£1.1m after only seven months with Celtic
in Scotland. He was a regular for his two
seasons at the club even though his goal
return wasn't brilliant. Left for Marseille
and he continued to play in France for
seven years. Since hanging up his boots
Cass has become a semi professional
poker player and a media pundit. Has
presented on Talksport, written for the
Times and Hot Press and as well as
making regular appearances on Sky
Sports.

## CASEY, Len, MBE

*Appearances: 37 Goals: 0 (1954-1958)*
*Career: Chelsea. Plymouth Argyle (1954-*
*1961).* Was one of a handful of players
recruited by Ted Drake out of the amateur
ranks Wasn't really considered to be a first
team regular except in 1957-1958 when
he made 24 appearances. Was sold to
Plymouth Argyle inn 1958 for £12,000 plus
Wally Bellett. Moved back to Essex and
spent 25 years working for Dagenham
Cables as a training officer until being
offered early retirement. He was awarded
an MBE for setting up an apprentice
scheme at the company. He also coached
the works' football team in the Essex
Business Houses Football League. These
days he lives in Benfleet but still attends
the Chelsea Pitch Owners dinner.

**Ricardo Carvalho.** *Photo: jspace3*

## CASIRAGHI, Pierluigi

*Appearances: 15  Goals: 1 (1998-2000)*
Career: *Chelsea. (1998-2002).* Cost The
Blues £5.4 million but the move turned out
to be a disaster. He suffered a cruciate
knee ligament injury in a collision with
West Ham keeper Shaka Hislop and ten
operations failed to save his career. He
returned to Italy to become Monza youth
coach, before taking charge of Serie C3
AC Legano. Since July 2006 has been
coach of the Italian under-21 side

## CASTLE, Sidney

*Appearances: 32  Goals: 2 (1923-1926)*
Career: *Tottenham Hotspur, Chelsea,
Charlton Athletic (1920-1926).* He could
operate on both flanks and spent three

years at Stamford Bridge which included a
relegation. He never settled into the team,
even though the same could be said for
the spells at any of his clubs. Ran a works
canteen in his native Basingstoke, where
he died in January 1978 aged 85.

## CHARVET, Laurent

*Appearances: 13  Goals: 2 (1998)*
Career: *Chelsea, Newcastle United,
Manchester City. (1998-2003).* A right
back signed on loan from Cannes. Was an
unused sub for the Cup Winners Cup
Final win over Stuttgart  but wasn't signed
on a permanent basis. He retired in 2004
after leaving Sochaux and has played pro-
poker and had property dealings.

## CHITTY, Wilf

*Appearances: 46  Goals: 16 (1930-1938)*
Career: *Chelsea, Plymouth Argyle,
Reading (1930-1948).* Became a loyal
servant in his eight seasons at Stamford
Bridge even though they were mainly
spent in the reserves. Scouted for
Chelsea, West Ham United and Reading.
Died in Berkshire in 1997.

## CHIVERS, Gary

*Appearances: 148  Goals: 4 (1978-1983)*
Career: *Chelsea, Swansea City, Queens
Park Rangers, Watford, Brighton,
Bournemouth. (1978-1995).* Signed for the
Blues on schoolboy forms before working
his way through the ranks making his first
team debut against Middlesbrough nine
months after turning professional. He went
from strength to strength in Geoff Hurst's
promotion chasing side in 1980 but he
played most of his games in blue as part
of the struggling Division Two side and it
resulted in a slump in form. He was
eventually allowed to leave for Swansea
City. These days lives in Epsom he works
as a football coach at a private school, and
has done PR and television work as well
as providing stats for the Press
Association. He also has a black cab
license.

**Gary Chivers**
*Photo: Rod George*

## CLARKE, Steve

*Appearances: 421  Goals: 10 (1987-1998)*
*Career: Chelsea.(1987-1998).* The right
back on Chelsea's team of the century,
cost £422,000 from St Mirren winning FA
Cup, League Cup and Cup Winners Cup
winners medals. The Cup Winners' Cup
final against Stuttgart was his last game
for the club. Moved to Newcastle as Ruud
Gullit's assistant before returning to
Stamford Bridge to work in a similar
capacity. Moved to West Ham to assist
Gianfranco Zola in September 2008, but
left in June 2010 following Zola's dismissal.

## CLEMENT, Neil

*Appearances: 4  Goals: 0 (1995-2000)*
*Career: Chelsea, Reading, Preston North
End, Brentford, West Bromwich Albion,
Hull City. (1996-2010).* His father Dave
was an England international and
stepfather Mike Kelly is Fulham's
goalkeeping coach. Made his Chelsea
debut against West Ham in December
1996, but struggled to make the break
through and was sold to WBA for
£150,000. Was forced to retire with a knee
injury and has since done some television
work for Sky.

## CLISS, David

*Appearances: 24  Goals: 1 (1956-1962)*
*Career: Chelsea (1956-1962).* An England
youth international who was an FA Youth
Cup finalist. Suffered a broken leg at the
start of the 1960-61and he never regained
his form, as a result was released into non
league football. He ran a window cleaning
business with Peter Sillett when they were
at Guildford City, only to find out they
were both afraid of heights when they
turned up to their first job! He emigrated
to Australia, where he died.

## COADY, John

*Appearances: 19  Goals: 3 (1986-1988)*
*Career: Chelsea (1986-1988).* The former
postman cost £35,000 from Shamrock

Rovers. He was 26 when he made his
debut against April 1987, scoring the only
goal in a 1-1 draw. Played either left back
or left side of midfield, but found it hard to
win a regular place in the team and was
released. Returned to Ireland where he
played for Derry City and Rovers again.
He still attends many of their games and
works as a postman.

## COCK, Jack

*Appearances: 110  Goals: 53 (1919-1923)*
*Career: Brentford, Huddersfield Town,
Chelsea, Everton, Plymouth Argyle,
Millwall. (1914-1931).* Signed for £2,500, a
fine athlete, who was two footed and
dangerous in the air, scored a goal every
two games. Starred in several films and
appeared in Music Hall's with his tenor
voice. Went onto manage Millwall and then
became the licensee in a New Cross pub,
died in Kensington in April 1966 aged 72.

## COLE, Carlton

*Appearances: 25  Goals: 4 (2001-2006)*
*Career: Chelsea, Wolves (loan), Charlton
Athletic (loan), Aston Villa (loan), West
Ham United (2001-2010.* Joined West Ham
in July 2006.

*Photo: East Ham Bull*

*Photo: Marathon Mitch*

## COLE, Joe

*Appearances: 183 Goals: 28 (2003-2010)
Career: West Ham United, Chelsea,
Liverpool (1998-2010).* Signed for
Liverpool on a free transfer in July 2010
and was promptly sent off on his League
debut against Arsenal.

## COLGAN, Nick

*Appearances 1 Goals: 0 (1992-1998)
Career: Chelsea, Crewe Alexandra,
Grimsby Town, Millwall, Brentford,
Reading, Bournemouth, Stockport County,
Barnsley, Ipswich Town, Grimsby Town.
(1992-2010).* Signed by Ian Porterfield as
back up to Dmitri Kharine and Kevin
Hitchcock. He needed several spells out on
loan to see any action before making his
only Chelsea appearance in a 3-2 defeat
against West Ham United in March 1997.
Was released on a free transfer by
Gianluca Vialli. A Republic of Ireland
international, Colgan has been playing for
Grimsby Town since 2009 and suffered
relegation to the Football Conference in 2010.

## COMPTON, John

*Appearances: 12 Goals: 0 (1955-1960)
Career: Chelsea, Ipswich Town,
Bournemouth. (1955-1965).* A wing half
who struggled to break past Derek
Saunders and Len Casey for a regular
game. He was released and became part
of the Ipswich team that won the First
Division title. Now lives in retirement in
Bournemouth. Drove a petrol tanker for
Texaco for 34 years before retiring, having
previously worked for Schweppes.

## COOKE, Charlie

*Appearances: 373 Goals: 30 (1966-1972
and 1974-1978) Career: Aberdeen,
Dundee, Chelsea, Crystal Palace,
Chelsea. (1959-1977).* One of the most
skillful players ever to have pulled on a
Chelsea shirt and is certainly one of the
most popular. A truly great entertainer
who played in four Cup Finals during his
ten years at Stamford Bridge. his Chelsea
career was split into two parts either side
of a 16 month stint at Crystal Palace. He
had arrived at the club as a direct
replacement for Terry Venables but was
moved to the wing to supply Tony Hateley.
Was the star of Chelsea's FA Cup victory
over Leeds and still had an impact when
the club won promotion seven years later
before heading off to America. He
developed a taste for American life which
tempted him to stay. Now lives in
Cincinnati, and runs a successful soccer
school.

## COPELAND, David

*Appearances 26 Goals: 9 (1905-1907)
Career: Tottenham Hotspur, Chelsea
(1899-1907).* Played in the Blues' first ever
fixture. Was appointed captain for their
second season, only to break his leg a few
months into the campaign. He was never
to play for the club again. Was working in
the Rose and Crown hotel in Erdington,
Birmingham at the time of his death from
heart failure in February 1931.

## CORTHINE, Peter

*Appearances: 2 Goals: 0 (1957-1960)*
Career: *Chelsea, Southend United. (1957-1960).* A winger who was spotted playing army football but he was unable to dislodge Peter Brabrook from the first team and was allowed to move to Southend. Worked as a maintenance foreman for Sun Life Assurance, later becoming a plumber until his retirement in 1993. He now lives in North London.

## COURT, Colin

*Appearances: 1 Goals: 0 (1954-1959)*
Career: *Chelsea, Torquay United (1954-1961).* Worked his way through the junior ranks, but with Eric Parsons and Peter Brabrook blocking his path to the first team he had to settle for one appearance against Frem in the Fairs Cup before being released. Later played for Torquay United and settled in South Devon. Now lives in retirement in Paignton.

## CRAWFORD, Jackie

*Appearances: 308 Goals: 27 (1923-1934)*
Career: *Hull City, Chelsea, Queens Park Rangers (1920-1937).* Joined from Hull City in 1923 for a fee of £3,000. Was signed as a right winger but was soon asked to switch to the left to make room for Alex Jackson. He went onto produce some outstanding displays and appeared in an all-star front line which included Hughie Gallacher, Alex Cheyne and Andy Wilson. An eternal optimist, Crawford was highly influential in the dressing. and it was a surprise that he did not win more than his one cap for England. This was gained in a defeat against Scotland in 1931. Coached QPR until 1939 and worked in a factory during the WW2. After the war he worked for Ford's in Dagenham until the 1960's. Died in September 1975, the day after his 79th birthday.

**Charlie Cooke** *Photo: thanks to James Hicks. Seen here with his father. They are both descended from James' great-great grandfather, F.W. Parker, one of the founders of Chelsea F.C*

Photo: Rechigi Park Hotel

## CRESPO, Hernan

*Appearances: 49  Goals: 20 (2003-2008)*
*Career: River Plate, Parma, Lazio,*
*Internazionale, Chelsea, Milan (loan),*
*Internazionale, Genoa, Parma (1993-2010.*
Argentinian Crespo, who was once a £16m
purchase, returned to Italian side Parma in
January 2010 - ten years after leaving the
Italian club.

## CRITTENDEN, Nick

*Appearances: 3  Goals: 0 (1997-2000)*
*Career: Chelsea, Plymouth Argyle, Yeovil.*
*(1997-2004).* The Blues' Young Player of
the Year in 1997 never looked like carving
out a career at Stamford Bridge because
of the amount of talent that the club had at
the time. Was allowed to join Yeovil on a
free transfer. Now works as a coach on
their Community scheme and still plays
non-league soccer for Dorchester Town.

## CROWTHER, Stan

*Appearances: 58  Goals: 0 (1958-1961)*
*Career: Aston Villa, Manchester United,*
*Chelsea, Brighton (1955-1961).* Arrived at
the Bridge for £10,000 in 1958 and
enjoyed two useful seasons at the club.
Was never in Tommy Doc's long term
plans and was sold to Brighton. Moved
back to his native Black Country after
quitting through disillusionment and
became a foreman at the Armitage Shanks
factory in Wolverhampton until retirement.

**Our site!** *www.where-are-they-now.co.uk*

Photo: Rod George

## CUDICINI, Carlo

*Appearances: 141  Goals: 0 (1999-2009)*
*Career: Milan, Como (loan), Prato, Lazio,*
*Castel di Sangro, Chelsea, Tottenham*
*Hotspur (1992-2010.)* Moved to Spurs on a
free transfer on 26th January 2009.

## CUNDY, Jason

*Appearances: 57  Goals: 2 (1988-1992)*
*Career: Chelsea, Tottenham Hotspur,*
*Crystal Palace, Bristol City, Ipswich Town,*
*Portsmouth. (1988-2000).* The Blues'
young player of the year in 1987, went
onto captain the reserves but could never
establish himself in the first team. The only
exception was the 1990-91 season, when
he partnered Ken Monkou in central
defence. He went on loan to Spurs in 1992
before sealing a £750,000 move. Since
being forced to retire through injury, he
has beaten cancer, coached at the
Chelsea academy,  and earns a living from
the media including a phone in with Scott

Minto on The Blues in-house television
channel. Has also worked for Sky TV and
Talksport Radio also ran an events
company with Clive Walker.

## DALLA BONA, Sam

*Appearances: 73  Goals: 6 (1998-2002)*
*Career: Chelsea. (1998-2002).* Signed
while captain of the Italian under-18 side.
He was Chelsea's Young Player of the Year
in 1998-99 after netting 16 goals for the
reserves but had to wait for Dennis Wise
and Gus Poyet to leave before getting an
extended run in the first team in 2001.
Things turned sour the next season when
he turned down the chance of a new
contract because he wanted to go home
to Italy and subsequently fell out with
Claudio Ranieri before securing a £1
million move to AC Milan. Has never
settled after leaving the club and has had
moves to Sampdoria and Napoli as well as
short term loans at Bologna, Lecce, Iraklis
in Greece and Vernona in 2010.

## D'ARCY, Jimmy

*Appearances: 31 Goals: 13 (1951-1952)*
*Career: Charlton Athletic, Chelsea,*
*Brentford. (1948-1953).* Cost the Blues
£10,000 and it looked to be a bargain
when he was joint top scorer with Roy
Bentley in his first season. However, he
was swapped with Ron Greenwood just a
few months into his second campaign.
Went onto become a liaison officer with
Charlton Athletic before working as a
machine operator for a glass company in
Sunbury, Surrey, where he was based until
his death in February 1985 aged 63.

## DAVIES, Gordon

*Appearances: 15 Goals: 6 (1984-1985)*
*Career: Fulham, Chelsea, Manchester*
*City, Fulham, Wrexham (1977- 1993).*
Nicknamed 'Ivor the Engine' because of
work rate following his £90,000 switch
from Fulham. A qualified teacher, he
worked as a PE instructor during his non
league days. Three of his six goals for the
Blues came against Everton at Goodison
Park, but he couldn't dislodge Kerry
Dixon and David Speedie and was sold to
Manchester City for £75,000 after less
than a year. After hanging up his boots,
Davies became a pest control officer for
Rentokil. Now runs his own pest control
company in Northamptonshire and does
corporate hospitality at Fulham games.

## DE GOEY, Ed

*Appearances: 179 Goals: 0 (1997-2003)*
*Career: Chelsea, Stoke City. (1997-2006).*
Became the most expensive goalkeeper
in the Premier League when The Blues
paid Feyenoord £2.25 million for his
services. He became first choice and
landed FA Cup, League Cup, Cup
Winners' Cup winners medals and kept a
then record 27 clean sheets in the 1999-
2000 season. Left for Stoke on a free
transfer after six seasons at Stamford
Bridge. Had a spell as QPR's goalkeeping
coach in 1997 but left after six months and
is still based in South East London.

**Ed de Goey** *Photo: ikoma*

## DE LUCAS, Enrique

*Appearances: 31 Goals: 1 (2002-2003)*
*Career: Chelsea. (2002-2003).* Spanish
midfielder Enrique "Quique" de Lucas
Martínez arrived at Stamford Bridge on a
four year contract in the summer of 2002
as one of the hottest properties in Le Liga.
Enjoyed a good first season with the club,
mainly playing on the right, and was
unlucky not to get a look in at the start of
the 2002/2003 season, before being
allowed to join Alaves on a free transfer.
Since 2009. He has since played mainly in
the second tier of Spanish football for
Murcia and Cartagena. His experiences at
Chelsea did not put him off these shores
altogether - he briefly returned to
England to have a trial with Blackpool in
August 2009. Has been a Celta Vigo
player since June 2010.

**GUESS WHO? - see page 150 for answers.** *Photo: Rod George*

Photo: toksuede

## DECO

Appearances: 43  Goals: 5 (2008-2010)
Career: Corinthians, Benfica, Alverca (loan), Salguerios (loan), Porton, Barcelona, Chelsea, Fluminese (1996-2010. Signed a two year contract with Brazilian side Fluminese in August 2010.

## DEL HORNO, Asier

Appearances: 34  Goals: 1 (2005-2006)
Career: Bilbao Athletic, Athletic Bilbao, Chelsea, Valencia, Athletico Bilbao (loan), (1999-2010). An £8 million purchase in 2005, Del Horno won a league winner's medal in his first season, but returned to Spain almost exactly a year after his arrival. Despite being registered as a Valencia player he spent the most of the 2009-2010 season on loan to Valladolid.

## DEMPSEY, John

Appearances: 207  Goals: 7 (1969-1978)
Career: Fulham, Chelsea, (1964-1975)..
Known as 'Mr Reliable', he became a pillar of strength in the middle of defence following his arrival at Stamford Bridge for £70,000 plus Barry Lloyd. Scored a vital goal in the Cup Winners' Cup replay victory over Real Madrid. His career was soon affected by a run of injury problems and went to America to end his career. Now works with adults who have learning difficulties at a daycentre in Barnet.

## DESAILLY, Marcel

Appearances: 222  Goals: 7 (1998-2004)
Career: Chelsea (1998-2004). Arrived at the Bridge from Milan for a well spent £4.6 million. Was recognised for much of his stay as the best in the world in his position formed a formidable partnership with Frank Leboeuf. He captained the team for four years, becoming a firm fans' favourite. Is now a Unicef ambassador for his native Ghana and works as a pundit for Canal Plus in France, as well as the BBC.

## DESCHAMPS, Didier

Appearances: 47  Goals: 1 (1999-2000)
Career: Chelsea (1999-2000). French football legend was once described as a 'water carrier' by Eric Cantona. Only spent one season at Stamford Bridge after leaving Juventus, when he helped the club to success in the 2000 FA Cup Final. Scored his only goal against Hertha Berlin in the Champions League. Left for Valencia after only one season before retiring. He has gone into management with Monaco, Juventus and since July 2009, another of his former clubs, Marseille.

**Marcel Desailly**
Photo: William Bedzrah

## DI MATTEO, Roberto

*Appearances: 175 Goals: 26 (1996-2002)*
*Career: Chelsea. (1996-2002).* A member of Chelsea's greatest ever XI, scored on his debut for The Blues against Middlesbrough. Scored after 42 seconds of the 1997 FA Cup Final against the same opposition -the quickest goal in a final at the old Wembley. In total, scored the winning goal in three finals before his career was ended by a broken leg. Opened a restaurant and worked in hospitality before going into management with MK Dons and since June 2009, West Bromwich Albion, leading them back into the Premier League in his first season.

## DIARRA, Lassana

*Appearances: 13 Goals: 0 (2005-2007)*
*Career: Le Havre, Chelsea, Arsenal, Portsmouth, Real Madrid (2003-2010).* Small but effective defensive midfielder who had arrived at Chelsea via Le Harve in 2005. Undoubtedly talented, he was sold to Arsenal in January 2008 before his contract expired, which would have allowed him to leave on a free transfer. Joined current club Real Madrid from Portsmouth for a reported £20 million in December 2008.

## DICKENS, Alan

*Appearances: 55 Goals: 4 (1989-1993)*
*Career: West Ham United, Chelsea, West Bromwich Albion, Brentford, Colchester United. (1982-1994).* Joined the Blues for £635,000 in August 1989, the second highest fee that the club paid for a player. He held his place until December but then over the next 12 months he had to make do with being on the fringes of the first team. In his second season with the club, had to wait until February for his first start. His career at the Bridge never hit the heights his talents deserved. The arrival of Vinnie Jones signalled the end of his stay and he was released on a free transfer, These days he lives in Barking and drives a London Cab for a living.

## DICKS, Alan

*Appearances: 38 Goals: 1 (1951-1958)*
*Career: Chelsea, Southend United, Coventry City. (1951-1962).* Was set to sign for Millwall when a Chelsea scout knocked on the door offering him £250 to move to Stamford Bridge instead. Over the next seven seasons he played understudy to Ken Armstrong, Stan Wicks and Derek Saunders. He played one game in the 1954-55 Championship winning season but was off-loaded along with Les Stubbs to Southend United for £12,000. Went into management with Bristol City and Fulham he then embarked on his travels, managing in five countries on three continents before retiring and moving back to Henleaze, Bristol.

## DICKSON, Bill

*Appearances: 119 Goals: 4 (1947-1953)*
*Career: Notts County, Chelsea, Arsenal, Mansfield Town (1946-1956).* Arrived at Stamford Bridge as a make-weight in part exchange for the great Tommy Lawton. In his first three seasons he was restricted to 19 appearances by a string of injuries but repaid the faith of Ted Drake in his final three seasons, chalking up 100 games. Drake then sold him to Arsenal for £15,000. He returned to live and work as scout for Arsenal in Lurgan, Northern Ireland, then worked as a joiner until retiring. Died in June 2002 aged 79.

## DIGWEED, Perry

*Appearances: 3 Goals: 0 (1988)*
*Career: Fulham, Brighton, WBA, Charlton Athletic, Newcastle United, Chelsea, Wimbledon, Watford. (1977-1994).* Signed by John Hollins on loan as cover for Roger Freestone after a serious injury ended the career of Eddie Niedzwiecki. He made three first team outings all of which ended in draws including a 4-4 and 3-3. These days, he has invested in property and runs an executive chauffeur business for racehorse owners.

**GUESS WHO? - see page 150 for answers.** *Photo: Rod George*

Photo: Rod George

# DIXON, Kerry

*Appearances: 420 Goals: 193 (1983-1992)*
Career: *Reading, Chelsea, Southampton, Luton Town, Millwall, Watford, Doncaster Rovers. (1980-1996).* A Blues legend who joined the club for £150,000 having made his name at Reading. He went from strength to strength after his move to Stamford Bridge in August 1983. A natural goalscorer, he netted 34 times in his first season. His first eight league goals for the club were all braces, and the club surged to the first of two Second Division titles in his time at the club. The next season he took the First Division by storm with 36 goals. A further £25,000 was paid out after he made his England debut and he snubbed the chance of joining Arsenal or West Ham for £1million to help the club to his second Division Two title in 1988-89. Over the next couple of seasons the goals started to dry up despite winning a Full Members Cup winners medal at Wembley against Middlesbrough in 1990 and within two years he was sold to Southampton for £575,000 with only Bobby Tambling having scored more goals for the club. Dixon ran a pub in Dunstable but these days is involved in events and match day hospitality for the Blues.

# DOCHERTY, Jim

*Appearances: 3 Goals: 0 (1979)*
Career: *Chelsea (1979).* A prolific scoring record for East Stirling persuaded the Blues to pay £45,000 in February 1979 to lure him South. The fee is still a club record for his former employers, but he never settled in the capital and struggled to find his feet in the Football League. Make only three first team appearances and by November he was sold to Dundee United. Having continued his career in Scotland, he now lives in Bathgate, West Lothian and is managing director of a successful drainage company Euro Environmental Contracts.

# DOCHERTY, Tommy

*Appearances 4 Goals: 0 (1961-1962)*
Career: *Celtic, Preston North End, Arsenal, Chelsea. (1948-1961).* 'The Doc' arrived at Stamford Bridge as a player/coach in 1961 but only played four games before retiring four months later. Within a year he had succeeded Ted Drake as manager and went about dismantling an aging team. He replaced the departing players with the likes of Terry Venables, Bobby Tambling, Peter Bonetti and Barry Bridges, who became known as 'Docherty's Diamonds'. Docherty won the League Cup and broke the club transfer record four times, but the death of Joe Mears in 1967 spelled the end of his stay at the club as he couldn't work with new chairman Charles Pratt junior. He then continued a colourful management career with Rotherham, QPR, Aston Villa, FC Porto, Hull City, the Scottish national side, Derby County, two Australian clubs, Preston North End and Altrincham, but only really enjoyed success at Manchester United. He retired from football management at the end of the 1987/8 season and has now spent over twenty years working as a successful media pundit and after dinner speaker.

## DODD, George

*Appearances: 31  Goals: 9 (1911-1913)*
*Career: Stockport County, Workington,*
*Notts County, Millwall, Chelsea Brighton,*
*Darlington, West Ham United, Luton*
*Town, Charlton Athletic. (1905-1922).*
Scored the first ever goal conceded by
the club while he was playing for
Stockport County. Then, seven years later,
was a member of the Chelsea side which
won promotion to the First Division. Lost a
large chunk of his career to the First War
World, but played on until 1922. Died in
1960

## DODDS, Billy

*Appearances: 5  Goals: 0 (1986-1989)*
*Career: Chelsea (1986-1989).* Is now seen
as 'one that got away' after a successful
career back in his native Scotland. Dodds
was a junior at the club and despite
scoring 27 goals in 30 games, he was only
given limited opportunities to impress at a
more senior level and struggled to make
the step up. Has been assistant manager
of Dundee since March 2010. Also works
as a media pundit for BBC Scotland and
the Scottish Sun. Has a keen interest in
horse racing and has owned several horses
with some success.

## DOLDING, Len

*Appearances: 27  Goals: 2 (1945-1948)*
*Career: Queens Park Rangers, Chelsea,*
*Norwich City (1943-1951).* A bomber pilot
during the Second World War, he was also
on the MMC ground staff for several
summers. As a cricketer, he played once
for Middlesex and acted as 12th man for
England in a test match. His football
career spanned eight years but he wasn't
able to establish himself in the Chelsea
team because of expensive signings like
Bobby Campbell, Johnny Paton and John
McInnes, and was sold to Norwich for
£2,000. Was sadly killed after a car crash
in Wembley, north London in November
1954 aged only 31.

## DONAGHY, Mal

*Appearances: 78  Goals: 3 (1992-1994)*
*Career: Luton Town, Manchester United,*
*Luton Town, Chelsea. (1978-1994).*
Signed for £100,000 just a month short of
his 35th birthday, so was very much in
twilight of his career at the club but gave
two seasons service alongside firstly Paul
Elliott and then David Lee. He then picked
up an injury against his former employers,
Manchester United, at Old Trafford and
never really recovered, having to retire on
medical grounds. Returned to his native
Northern Ireland where he has worked for
the Northern Irish FA in a number of
development roles since 2000.

## DORIGO, Tony

*Appearances: 180  Goals: 12 (1987-1991)*
*Career: Aston Villa, Chelsea, Leeds*
*United, Derby County, Stoke City. 1983-*
*2000.* An Australian who became an
England international. Moved to Stamford
Bridge from Aston Villa in a £475,000 deal,
and soon proved to be something of a
bargain signing, winning the club Player
of the Year award after forming a
formidable partnership full back with
partnership with Steve Clarke in his first
season. Later had three written transfer
requests rejected by Bobby Campbell
because he was worried about his
international chances, but he eventually
agreed to honour his four-year contract. A
majestic player with the ball at his feet, he
was equally able from a set piece - his
free kick winning the 1990 ZDS Cup
against Middlesbrough at Wembley. He
was also a Second Division Championship
winner in 1989 but as soon as his contract
was up, Dorigo agreed to join Leeds
United for a tribunal settled fee of £1.3
million. Since retiring, he has done some
work as a television pundit but these days
lives in Hartford, Cheshire, running a
property company Premiership
Developments which has offices in
Manchester and the Algarve.

**GUESS WHO (*) - see page 150 for answers.** *Photo: Dan Davies*

### DONALD, Alexander

*Appearances: 24 Goals: 1 (1930-1932)*
Career: *Chelsea, Bristol Rovers. (1930-1936)*. A Scotsman signed from American side New York Nationals and spent two seasons at the club, Returned to his roots north of the border, after the war to coach the Kirkintilloch Boy Club. Died in 1949

### DOUGLAS, Angus

*Appearances: 103 Goals: 11 (1908-1913)*
Career: *Chelsea, Newcastle United. (1907-1914)*. Chose a move to Chelsea ahead of Everton when he moved south from a local club in his native Lochmaben. Took half a season to settle but soon became a firm favourite with the Stamford Bridge faithful. Survived the First World War only to die in the national flu pandemic of December 1918.

### DOW, Andy

*Appearances: 18 Goals: 0 (1993-1996)*
Career: *Chelsea, Bradford City (1993-1996)*. Was signed by Glenn Hoddle from Dundee for £250,000 in July 1993 on the recommendation of youth team Graham Rix, who had spent some time in Scotland. His career at The Bridge proved to be a stop start affair and he was in and out of the first team as they reached the FA Cup Final. The arrivals Dan Petrescu and Terry Phelan saw him sold to Hibs for £125,000. Dow is still playing local football in Scotland and is running a pub in Dundee.

### DOWNING, Sam

*Appearances: 144 Goals: 10 (1909-1914)*
Career: *QPR, Chelsea. (1903-1914)*. A powerful wing half who was a key member of the Chelsea team for four years and was a firm favourite with the Stamford Bridge faithful after signing from QPR. Captained the side on a number of occasions until his career was cut short by the outbreak of World War One. Lived in North London and later coached cricket at a school in Maidenhead.

**Phil Driver**

### DRIVER, Phil

*Appearances: 46 Goals: 4 (1980-1983)*
Career: *Luton Town, Wimbledon, Chelsea, Wimbledon. (1977-1985)*. Signed by Geoff Hurst for £20,000 because he was looking for some width on the right wing. Driver being a good crosser with neat skills and good pace seemed to fit the bill and certainly his early contributions sparked a revival in the clubs fortunes. A knee injury suffered at Cambridge was the beginning of the end for his Blues career - when he returned, he struggled to rediscover his early promise and was allowed to return to Wimbledon. Lives in Welwyn Garden City and is club captain for the local cricket club. Worked for Blue Arrow Recruitment before entering the hospitality industry, firstly with Ambro Events and now the Cavendish Group.

## DROY, Micky

*Appearances: 313 Goals: 19 (1970-1985)*
*Career: Chelsea, Luton Town, Crystal
Palace, Brentford. (1970-1986).* Tower of
strength upon which many a Chelsea
defence was structured. He arrived from
non league Slough Town as a 19 year-old
where he had learned his trade and
became one of the sturdiest defenders
around in the 1970's. For much of his fifteen
years in SW6 there was turmoil both on and
off the pitch. He suffered two relegations
from the First Division and was part of the
team that narrowly avoided relegation to the
Third Division. While off the pitch, the club
was in a pickle and financial disaster was
never far away. Was voted Player of the Year
in 1978 and spent four years as captain but
after the signing Joe McLaughlin he found
himself released to join Crystal Palace. He
ran a successful electrical wholesale
business in Kensal Green for many years
but has now moved to Florida.

**Keith Dublin.** *Photo: Rod George*

## DUBLIN, Keith

*Appearances: 68 Goals: 0 (1983-1987)*
*Career: Chelsea, Brighton & Hove Albion,
Watford, Southend United, Colchester
United. (1984-1998).* Was voted Young
Player of the Year in 1983 made his debut
in the final game of the Second Division
title winning season in1983/84 against
Barnsley. He then had to wait until the
following March for his First Division bow
against Spurs Was never really able to
take the number three shirt away from
Doug Rougvie until 1986/87, when he
formed an impressive full back
partnership with Steve Clarke. The
arrivals of Clive Wilson and Tony Dorigo
signalled the end of his time at Stamford
Bridge and he was sold to Brighton for
£35,000. Since retiring, he has been living
in Surbiton, Surrey and has worked in IT,
the family property management business
and is keen sports motivational speaker.

## DUDLEY, Sam

*Appearances: 1 Goals: 0 (1932-1934)*
*Career: Preston, Bournemouth, Clapton
Orient, Chelsea, Exeter City. (1927-1935).*
Dudley only had one outing as a wing half
in a match against Newcastle United in
February 1933. His brother Jimmy was on
the books of West Bromwich Albion. Died
in Dudley, Staffordshire in January 1985,

## DUFFY, Bernard

*(1923-1927)*
*Career: Chelsea, Clapton Orient (1923-
1929).* A wing half who never established
himself in four seasons at the club despite
being a near ever present for the
reserves. He was unable to dislodge
fellow-Scotsman Jock Priestly and was
allowed to move across London to Clapton
Orient in 1927. After playing in Ireland, he
returned to his Scottish homeland and
worked for a Hamilton bookmaker. In later
life he was an avid follower of Celtic. Died
in Glasgow in 1970.

## DUNN, John

*Appearances: 16 Goals: 0 (1962-1966)*
Career: *Chelsea, Torquay United, Aston Villa, Charlton Athletic. (1962-1975).*
Signed from Essex Schools, he became the understudy to Peter Bonetti after the departure of Errol McNally. Accordingly, he found his chances limited despite being a competent and brave keeper. Dunn left for Torquay United on a free transfer in 1966 and later played for Aston Villa and Charlton. Now lives in Basildon, Essex and works as a PE teacher in Barking Abbey Sports College having worked a various other schools in the area since hanging up his boots.

## DURIE, Gordon

*Appearances: 153 Goals: 63 (1986-1991)*
Career: *Chelsea, Tottenham Hotspur. (1986-1993).* Jukebox' was a folk hero at Hibs when The Blues paid £380,000 in April 1986 to tempt him south. He struggled at first but as soon as he struck up a prolific partnership with Kerry Dixon the goals flowed including five in game against Walsall in February 1989. His five year stay came to an end when Durie claimed he wanted to move back north to be nearer to his and his wife's families. He ended up moving no further than Tottenham in north London. He now lives in retirement in Dulgery Bay after finishing his career with Rangers in 2000.

## DYKE, Charles

*Appearances: 25 Goals: 2 (1947-1951)*
Career: *Chelsea (1947-1951).* Had to battle Bobby Campbell for a place in the Chelsea forward line during his four years at the club. Made his debut against Aston Villa at Villa Park in February 1948 but was mainly a reserve. Returned to his native Barry where he continues to live in retirement after working for the local council maintaining parks and bowling greens. He also worked behind the bar in Barry Town's social club which his wife ran.

## Edwards, Robert

*Appearances: 13 Goals: 2 (1951-1955)*
Career: *Chelsea, Swindon Town, Norwich City, Northampton Town. (1951-1961).*
Signed for the Blues after he completed his National Service, and spent four years at the club without really making a break through and with his chances limited in Ted Drake's title winning side he was sold to Swindon for £2,000. Returned to the Norwich area after retirement and worked as a milkman.

**Paul Elliott supporting England's bid to host the 2018 World Cup finals.**
*Photo courtesy of England 2018 Bid*

## ELLIOTT, Paul, MBE

*Appearances: 54 Goals: 3 (1991-1994)*
Career: *Charlton Athletic, Luton Town, Aston Villa, Chelsea. (1981-1994).* Paul was Chelsea's Player of the Year and had formed a solid partnership with Ken Monkou when, in 1992, aged 28, his career was ended as a result of a tackle from Liverpool's Dean Saunders. He lost a subsequent court case, and faced court costs of around £500,000. Became a T.V. pundit, worked in Chelsea's sponsorship department, became an advisor to the Equality and Human Rights Commission, and was a member of the FA's bid for the 2018 World Cup. His work with youngsters and active campaigning against racism in the game was rewarded in 2003, when he was awarded the MBE.

**GUESS WHO?** - see page 150 for answers. *Photo: Rowan*

## ELLIOT, Sidney

*Appearances: 30  Goals: 9 (1928-1930)*
*Career: Durham City, Fulham, Chelsea, Bristol City, Notts County, Bradford City, Rochdale. (1926-1935).* A typical centre forward who arrived at The Bridge from local neighbours Fulham for a record fee of £3,600. He went to work for FB Minter Sports and played for the works team. Died in Gravesend, Kent in September 1986 aged 78.

## ELMES, Timmy

*Appearances: 4  Goals: 0 (1980-1981)*
*Career: Chelsea, Leyton Orient. (1980-1981).* Tough in the tackle, he never hit the heights expected of him after doing well in intermediate football and was released after just a handful of appearances. Went onto play for Redhill with more success and is now living in the Croydon area

## EVANS, Bobby

*Appearances: 37  Goals: 1 (1960-1961)*
*Career: Chelsea, Newport County. (1961-1962).* A legend North of the Border by the time The Blues paid £12,000, even though he was clearly past his best. At 33, he still managed to give the club a season's good service before leaving to become the player manager of Newport County. He once acted as a back up singer to Bing Crosby during a pre season tour with Celtic when they were travelling on the same ship. Returned to Scotland where he died in September 2001 aged 74 in Cumbernauld, after suffering from Parkinson's disease.

## FAIRGRAY, Norman

*Appearances: 84  Goals: 5 (1907-1914)*
*Career: Lincoln City, Chelsea. (1903-1914).* A clever but inconsistent winger, who spent seven years at the club. Didn't play the number of games that his popularity with the crowd demanded. Returned to Scotland to live in Dumfries where he worked in a motor works died in the mid-1950s.

## FALCO, Mark

*Appearances: 3  Goals: 0 (1982)*
*Career: Tottenham Hotspur, Chelsea, Watford, Rangers, Queens Park Rangers, Millwall (1978-1991).* Was signed on a month's loan from Spurs in November 1982 and played three games without finding the target. Is now a partner in a cleaning and asbestos clearing business in Hertfordshire with former Spurs team mate John Pratt.

## FASCIONE, Joe

*Appearances: 34  Goals: 1 (1962-1969)*
*Career: Chelsea (1962-1969).* He had six seasons at the club but is most famous as one of the eight players sent home from Blackpool by Tommy Docherty for breaking a pre-match curfew in April 1965. Was given a second chance by Dave Sexton but couldn't reproduce his form in front of goal. Worked as a salesman for former Crystal Palace chairman Ray Bloye alongside John Edrich, did various other clubs including working for the Savoy Group and was a mini cab driver in Surrey before moving to Pagham near Bognor Regis.

## FEELY, Peter

*Appearances: 5  Goals: 2 (1970-1973)*
*Career: Chelsea, Bournemouth, Fulham, Gillingham, Sheffield Wednesday, Stockport County (1970-1977).* Signed professional terms three days after scoring for Enfield in their 1970 Amateur Cup Final success, and then scored on a league debut against Coventry City on April 1971. He then found challenging Peter Osgood, Ian Hutchinson and Tommy Baldwin for a regular place an almost impossible task and was sold to Bournemouth for a £1,000. After hanging up his boots he went to live in the Far East where he became a quantity surveyor and also bought and sold land becoming a multi-millionaire, is now based in Perth, Western Australia.

## FERGUSON, Willie

*Appearances: 294 Goals: 11 (1921-1933)*
Career: *Chelsea (1921-1933)*. Ferguson is considered to be one of the Blues all-time greats. He started his career at the club as a centre forward before moving back to wing half, where he became first choice for almost a decade. A terrier-like player, he suffered a relegation and won a promotion. Returned to Scotland where he lived in Dumfries running a tobacconists until his death in August 1960 aged 59.

## FERRER, Albert

*Appearances: 113 Goals: 1 (1998-2003)*
Career: *Chelsea (1998-2003)*. Became a 'Mr Reliable' following his £2.2 million switch from Barcelona. An Olympic Gold medallist, he was part of the first ever Chelsea team to qualify for the Champions League but did miss out on two FA Cup Final appearances through injury and non selection. He retired at the age of 33 in May 2003 when his contract expired. Disappeared from view for a few years but is now regularly seen on Sky as a pundit for their coverage of Spanish football.

**Steve Finnieston.** *Photo: Rod George*

## FERRIS, James

*Appearances: 39 Goals: 9 (1920-1922)*
Career: *Chelsea, Preston North End (1920-1924)*. Arrived in London with a big reputation following a decade playing in Northern Ireland but he never settled in the capital and left after two years. He eventually returned to Belfast but his career was ended through ill health in May 1930 after being diagnosed with a heart condition. Was working as a scout for Celtic before he died in 1932 aged just 37, his son Ray later became an international.

## FILLERY, Michael

*Appearances: 181 Goals: 41 (1978-1983)*
Career: *Chelsea, Queens Park Rangers, Portsmouth, Oldham Athletic, Millwall, Torquay United (1978-1992)*. A highly talented midfielder with a cultured left foot. He scored for the first goal of the 1980's away at Luton and scored some spectacular goals, including one against Spurs in an FA Cup quarter final and a 35 yard stunner away at Orient. His progress wasn't helped by the turmoil the club was in during his four years as a first team regular. It was the need for cash that facilitated his £200,000 sale to QPR in 1983. He became a TV presenter/pundit with Channel East and has also worked on Chelsea TV as well as being a school maintenance manager in North London.

## FINNIESTON, Steve

*Appearances: 90 Goals: 37 (1971-1978)*
Career: *Chelsea, Cardiff City, Sheffield United. (1971-1979)*. Edinburgh born striker, nicknamed 'Jock', became a regular in the 1976-77 promotion winning season, scoring 24 goals including a hat trick on the final day against Hull City. An Achilles tendon injury caused him to miss much of the following season and he was forced to retire aged just 25. Worked as a postman, then became a full-time sales rep for builders merchants Travis Perkins. Is now self-employed sales rep.

## FLECK, Robert

*Appearances: 48 Goals: 4 (1992-1995)*
*Career: Norwich City, Chelsea, Bolton Wanderers, Bristol City, Norwich City, Reading. (1987-1999).* Arrived at Stamford Bridge for £2.1million in August 1992 after a prolific spell at Norwich. His stint in West London wasn't to be as successful with the goals not flowing as freely. He struggled to fit in, especially as the style of play didn't really suit him. He was popular with fans and was immortalised in the song 'We all live in a Robert Fleck World' to a tune of the Beatles' Yellow Submarine. After retiring he ran his own soccer school, coached local non league teams and scouted part time for Norwich. He is now a teaching assistant in the town

Tore Andre Flo.

## FLO, Tore Andre

*Appearances: 149 Goals: 50 (1997-2000)*
*Career: Sogndal, Tromso, Brann, Chelsea, Rangers, Sunderland, Siena, Valerenga, Leeds United, Milton Keynes Dons (1993-2009).* Retired from the game in March 2008, but old team-mate Roberto Di Matteo lured him back to play for Milton Keynes Dons in the following November. Left the club in May 2009.

## FORREST, Craig

*Appearances: 3 Goals: 0 (1997)*
*Career: Ipswich Town, Colchester United, Chelsea, West Ham United. (1985-2002).* Arrived on loan and played three games. The Blues tried to sign him permanently but the bid was turned down by the Ipswich board. Was forced to retire after complications arising from testicular cancer, returned home to Canada where he works as a sports analyst for Rogers Sportsnet and CBC

## FORSELL, Mikael

*Appearances: 33 Goals: 5 (1998-2005)*
*Career: HJK, Chelsea, Crystal Palace (loan), Borussia Monchengladbach (loan), Birmingham City, Hannover 96 (1997-2010).* Mikael has been playing in Germany for Hannover 96 since 2008.

## FOSS, Dick

*Appearances: 48 Goals: 3 (1936-1952)*
*Career: Thames Association, Tottenham Hotspur, Chelsea (1931-1951).* A crucial figure in the history of Chelsea FC. He arrived from non league Southall after going unnoticed by other London clubs and was only one of three players to play for the club on either side of the Second World War. During the conflict he was working in London and was a regular in the half back line but when hostilities ended he struggled to hold on a regular place. In 1952 he was appointed manager of the club's youth policy which he had started five years earlier and in doing so had created a production line that was to develop legends like Venables, Greaves, Osgood, Tambling and Bonetti. He stayed in the job until the late 1960's and lived in London until his death in 1991.

## FOULKE, Willie

*Appearances: 35 Goals: 0 (1905-1906)*
*Career: Sheffield United, Chelsea, Bradford City. (1894-1907).* 'Fatty' Foulke is one of the football's legendary figures thanks to his 25 stone frame. He arrived at the club in their first ever league season for £50. It is said that he put on two stone during his one season at the club. Popular with fans, he is probably Chelsea's first ever superstar. Despite his bulk, he also managed to play county cricket for Derbyshire. After retiring he had a number of business interests in Sheffield including a shop and a pub prior to his death in May 1916. He is buried in Burngreave Cemetery.

## FRANCIS, Steve

*Appearances: 88 Goals: 0 (1981-1987)*
*Career: Chelsea, Reading, Huddersfield Town, Northampton Town. (1981-1997).* Essex born goalkeeper, signed as an apprentice in July 1980 but didn't have to wait that long for his first team debut. This came against Southampton in October 1981 when John Neal's patience with Petar Borota finally snapped and Francis then enjoyed a two year run in the first team, clocking up 73 consecutive appearances. The arrival of Eddie Niedzwiecki saw him lose his place and it wasn't to be until 1986 that he would get another run in the team this time seven games including the Full Members Cup Final, which he picked up a winners medal but he didn't have the confidence of John Hollins and was sold to Reading for £50,000. After retiring he married into a rich family is a postman in Henley in Arden, Warwickshire.

## FREEMAN, Charlie

*Appearances: 105 Goals: 22 (1907-1920)*
*Career: Fulham, Chelsea, Gillingham (1907- 1922).* Signed as a professional at the age of 20 but had to wait two years for his league debut against Sunderland at Roker Park, but was never classed as a first choice player and missed out on selection for the 1915 FA Cup Final, but his career at the club spanned both world wars. He returned to the club in 1923 as an odd job man and then became first team trainer during the second world war and then groundsman before retiring in 1953. He died in Fulham in March 1956.

Mikael Forsell.

## FREESTONE, Roger

*Appearances: 53 Goals: 0 (1987-1991)*
Career: *Newport County, Chelsea, Swansea City, Hereford, United, Swansea City. (1986-2004).* Moved to Stamford Bridge for around £95,000 after playing only 14 first team games for Newport. He soon found himself thrust into first team action because of injuries. A safe pair of hands for the four years he spent at the Bridge although he never quite established himself as first choice despite playing over 50 games. Helped the club to the Second Division title in 1989 but was allowed to leave by Bobby Campbell after falling behind Dave Beasant and Kevin Hitchcock in the fight for the first team jersey. Now works as a delivery driver for a parcel company.

## FRIDGE, Les

*Appearances: 1 Goals: 0 (1985-1987)*
Career: *Chelsea (1985-1987).* Highly rated in Scotland, he let five goals in against Watford on his only first team appearance. Returned to north of the border after failing to dislodge Eddie Niedzwiecki and Tony Godden from the team. Coached Inverness CT's youth team briefly and has been manager of Highland League Nairn County since 2004, where he is employed full time by the club.

## FROST, Lee

*Appearances: 15 Goals: 5 (1976-1980)*
Career: *Chelsea, Brentford (1976-1981).* A speedy winger appeared to be heading for the top after spending four promising seasons in the youth and reserve teams, but he never made the step up despite a hat trick in the 7-3 win over Leyton Orient in November 1977. Was sold to Brentford for £15,000 after a loan spell but drifted out of the game in the same season. Became an HGV lorry driver working for Pickfords in Horsham, Sussex.

## FURLONG, Paul

*Appearances: 85 Goals: 17 (1994-96)*
Career: *Coventry City, Watford, Chelsea, Birmingham City, Queens Park Rangers, Sheffield United, Queens Park Rangers, Luton Town, Southend United, Barnet. (1991-2010).* Signed for a club record £2.4 million in May 1994 and in his first season at Stamford Bridge helped the club reach the semi finals of the Cup Winners Cup only to lose out to Barcelona. He then found his chances limited by the arrivals of Ruud Gullit and Mark Hughes and when Gianluca Vialli pitched up he opted to drop down a division and sign for Birmingham City. Was released by Barnet at the end of the 2009-10 season and returned to non-league football to join Kettering Town as a player-coach.

## GALLAGHER, Hughie

*Appearances: 144 Goals: 81 (1930-1934)*
Career: *Newcastle United, Chelsea, Derby County, Notts County, Grimsby Town, Gateshead (1921-1939).* One of the games true immortals, Gallagher was Chelsea's first ever £10,000 signing. Newcastle originally rejected the Blues' approach but, when they finally relented, it sparked protests outside St James Park that lasted two weeks. He immediately settled at the club thanks to fellow Scottish internationals Andy Wilson and Tommy Law. Despite being put up in digs at Barons Court he went on and gave the club four and a half years of excellent service. His record speaks for itself but in the end his personal life took its toll. Drink and marital problems coupled with the fact that he was said to be heavily in debt after a divorce caused much distress. He tried several jobs after retiring, one of them being a sports journalist. However following the sudden death of his wife, and several family feuds, Gallacher took his own life by jumping in front of an express train in 1957. He was 54 years old.

**GUESS WHO?** - see page 150 for answers. *Photo: Rod George*

## GALLAS, William

*Appearances: 159  Goals: 14 (2001-2006)*
Career: *Caen, Marseille, Chelsea, Arsenal Tottenham Hotspur. (1995-2010).* Played for Arsenal until the end of the 2009/10 season but he and the club could not agree financial terms on a new contract. As a free agent, agreed to join Tottenham Hotspur in August 2010.

## GARLAND, Chris

*Appearances: 114  Goals: 31 (1971-1975)*
Career: *Bristol City, Chelsea, Leicester City, Bristol City. (1966-1982).* Admits that he signed a blank contract when he joined the Blues in a £100,000 deal from Bristol City and didn't realise that the rise in wages still didn't cover the cost of living in London. Was signed as cover for Peter Osgood, Tommy Baldwin and Ian Hutchinson, but he still saw his fair share of action averaging a goal in almost every four games. The highlights were scoring in both legs of the 1972 League Cup semi final against Spurs to earn a Wembley date with Stoke. After being sold to Leicester for £95,000, he helped keep his new club in the First Division at the expense of his former employers. Has had many jobs outside the game. Ventures in the fruit-and-veg business and then in the wine trade proved unsuccessful, while a career in insurance ended in redundancy. A gambling problem led to a marriage break-up and bankruptcy. At one stage he was reported to be homeless and sleeping rough but is now living in Newport, Wales.

## GARNER, Bill

*Appearances: 119  Goals: 36 (1972-1978)*
Career: *Notts County, Southend United, Chelsea, Cambridge United, Brentford. (1966-1984).* A traditional centre forward who impressed Dave Sexton enough that he paid £100,000 for him. He was dogged by injuries throughout his career but his scoring record was sufficiently impressive to attract the interest of England boss Don Revie when he named an enormous 84 man squad of players good enough to play international football, he never won a cap however. Bill became a school teacher and has run coaching courses for kids during the holidays and coached at Southend's Centre of Excellence.

## GIBBS, Derek

*Appearances: 25  Goals: 6 (1955-1960)*
Career: *Chelsea, Leyton Orient, Queens Park Rangers. (1955-1964).* His career almost never got off the ground as it was feared he would never play again after crushing his foot in an accident at work as a 15 year-old. Happily, he recovered and joined the Blues as a junior, making his league debut five years later. Was never able to establish himself in the team with the likes of Jimmy Greaves ahead of him and was allowed to leave for Leyton Orient where he enjoyed success. Worked for Securicor and then in a quarry in near his home in Porthcawl for 28 years. Died suddenly in November 2009 aged 74

**William Gallas** *Photo: Tapdown*

## GILKES, Michael

*Appearances: 2 Goals: 0 (1992)*
*Career: Reading, Chelsea, Southampton,*
*Wolverhampton Wanderers,*
*Millwall.(1984-1991).* A loan signing from
Reading in January and February 1992.
Made just one substitute appearance in
the league but had more success with
Southampton, Wolves and Millwall. Ran a
Football Academy at Newbury College,
but is now a Mortgage Consultant for a
Reading based Estate Agent

## GODDARD, Ray

*Appearances: 15 Goals: 1 (1946-1948)*
*Career: Wolverhampton Wanderers,*
*Chelsea, Plymouth Argyle, Exeter City*
*(1938-1954).* A useful player who could
play anywhere in the half back line and
made his debut in a 7-4 defeat to
Liverpool at Anfield. Finished his career
in the West Country with Exeter City and
then returned home to the West Midlands.
Lived and worked in Dudley until his
death in February 1974 aged 53.

## GODDEN, Tony

*Appearances: 38 Goals: 0 (1986-1987)*
*Career: West Bromwich Albion, Luton*
*Town, Walsall, Chelsea, Birmingham City,*
*Bury, Peterborough United. (1976-1989).*
Initially signed on loan by John Hollins in
March 1986 when Eddie Niedzwiecki was
injured and Steve Francis lost form. He
performed well enough to be signed
permanently at the start of next season and
within weeks, enjoyed the highlight of his
stay, saving two penalties in front of the
Stretford End to help earn a 1-0 win over
Manchester United. Injuries and illness
prevented progress and when Roger
Freestone was signed, Godden never
regained his first team slot. Went on to play
for three more clubs before turning his hand
to coaching keepers for a living. Has served
as coach to a number of League clubs has
also managed non league Kings Lynn FC. Is
now on Brighton's coaching staff.

Photo: WallyG

## GOLDBAEK, Bjarne

*Appearances: 40 Goals: 5 (1998-2000)*
*Career: Chelsea, Fulham. (1998-2003).*
Impressed after scoring twice against the
Blues in a Cup Winners' Cup tie for
Copenhagen and joined the club for
£350,000 plus fellow Dane Brian Laudrop.
A strong right sided midfielder, he could
slot in a right back and had a powerful
shot. Initially made a big impression at the
Bridge but then couldn't get a regular run
of games because of Gianluca Vialli's
rotation policy and he was sold to Fulham.
Since retiring in 2005, he has worked as a
pundit on Danish television, is a registered
agent and has passed his managers exam
in Germany, where he also advises FC
Schalke on players.

## GOULDEN, Len

*Appearances: 111 Goals: 19 (1945-1950)*
*Career: West Ham United, Chelsea.*
*(1933-1950).* Len Goulden was signed for £5,000 to partner Tommy Lawton just before the end of the Second World War. His career would have reached even greater heights had it not have been for Hitler's march into Poland. He was considered to be one of the greatest inside forwards of his day and was a bargain signing, having helped The Blues win the Football League Southern Cup as a guest. Gave superb service in five years, before retiring. He went on to manage Watford twice, coached in Libya, ran a sub post office, worked on a US Air Force base in Northampton before coaching Oxford United. He died in Cornwall in February 1995 aged 82.

## GRAHAM, George

*Appearances: 102 Goals: 46 (1964-1966)*
*Career: Aston Villa, Chelsea, Arsenal, Manchester United, Portsmouth, Crystal Palace. (1962-1977).* Signed for £5,000 in July 1964, 'Stroller' formed a deadly partnership with Barry Bridges and scored a goal every two games. Superb in the air, he was also a provider for Bridges and Bobby Tambling. Although part of the 1965 League Cup winning team, he eventually clashed with Tommy Docherty and was one of eight players sent home for breaking a pre match curfew. Was sold to Arsenal for £75,000 plus Tommy Baldwin in 1966 just six weeks after having a transfer request refused. Managed Millwall and Arsenal before being banned for accepting an "unsolicited gift". Went onto to take charge of Leeds and Spurs but is now a media pundit.

**George Graham & Terry Venables.** *Photo: Commander Idham*

## GRANVILLE, Danny

*Appearances: 26 Goals: 1 (1997-1998)*
*Career: Cambridge United, Chelsea, Leeds United, Manchester City, Norwich City, Crystal Palace, Colchester United. Leyton Orient. (1996-2009).* Attracted the interest of a number of top clubs when he was at Cambridge United but chose to join the Blues in a £300,000 deal. Became first choice left back until Graeme Le Saux returned from Blackburn Rovers from which time he was more of a a bit part player. Still took part in the 1998 Cup Winners' Cup Final success before leaving for Leeds United in a £1.6 million deal. He joined Hemel Hempstead Town in October 2009.

*Photo: www.sport-memorabilia.co.uk*

## GREAVES, Jimmy

*Appearances: 169 Goals: 132 (1957-1961)*
*Career: Chelsea, Tottenham Hotspur, West Ham United. (1957-1970).* One of the most lethal goal scorers in English football history, his scoring record for the club is second to none, 132 goals in 169 games. Finished as leading scorer in each of the four seasons that he spent in the Blues first team The 41 goals that he scored in the 1960-1961 season is still a club record.

Scored five goals in a game three times during his stay in SW6 and his £80,000 sale to AC Milan in June 1961 sparked protests which were long and hard from Chelsea fans. However, with the maximum wage in force in English football at the time the clubs hands were tied. After recovering from alcoholism he formed a successful double act with Ian St John on television as 'Saint & Greavsie'. Is still in demand as a newspaper columnist and after dinner speaker.

## GRAY, Billy

*Appearances: 172 Goals: 15 (1949-1953)*
*Career: Wolves, Leyton Orient, Chelsea, Burnley, Notts Forest, Millwall. (1944-1964).* A fast clever winger, he quickly settled following his free transfer from Orient. Spent four years at Stamford Bridge, becoming a first team regular and playing in two losing FA Cup semi-finals. Managed Millwall, Brentford and Notts County, coached at Fulham then became groundsman at the City Ground before owning a shop in Wollaton for many years. Now lives in retirement in Aspley.

## GREGG, Bob

*Appearances: 51 Goals: 6 (1933-1938)*
*Career: Darlington, Sheffield Wednesday, Birmingham City, Chelsea. (1926-1938).* Arrived at Stamford Bridge aged 29 with his best years behind him. Never really settled at the club and spent the majority of his time in the reserves. He died in Hounslow in May 1991 aged 87.

## GRODAS, Frode

*Appearances: 27 Goals: 1 (1996-1998)*
*Career: Chelsea, Tottenham. (1996-1998).* A Norwegian goalkeeper, signed on a free transfer. he played in the 1997 FA Cup Final victory over Middlesbrough but returned home in 2006. Was appointed manager of Ham-Kam but only lasted a season Was the goalkeeping coach at Lillestrøm SK. Grodas is now helping the keepers of the Norwegian national team.

Photo: Louise Haigh

## GREENWOOD, Ron

*Appearances: 66 Goals: 0 (1940-1945 and 1952-1955).* Career: *Chelsea, Bradford Park Avenue, Brentford, Chelsea, Fulham. (1940-1955).* Joined the club as an amateur guest in 1940 before turning professional three years later. Was allowed to leave on a free transfer, only to return seven years later in the latter stages of his career. He went on to become a member of Ted Drake's 1955 Championship winning side, playing every game until Christmas. After this he lost his centre half spot to Stan Wicks and was released for a second time at the end of the season. Was assistant manager of Arsenal before making his name at West Ham as manager and then general manger. He was then appointed England manager in 197,7 staying in the role until 1982. A spell as a director at Brighton followed before going on to work on BBC Radio. Lived in retirement in Sudbury, Suffolk until his death in February 2006 aged 84 after a long battle with Alzheimer's disease.

## GRONKJAER, Jesper

*Appearances: 119 Goals: 11 (2000-2004)* Career: *Chelsea, Birmingham City. (2000-2005).* Signed for £7.8 million from Ajax in December 2000, a fast skillful winger, was the most expensive Danish player in history. However, he was inconsistent and was sold to Birmingham City by Jose Mourinho. He has been playing for FC Copenhagen since 2006.

*Photo: Sylvia Gutiérrez*

## GUDJOHNSEN, Eidur

*Appearances: 182 Goals: 54 (2000-2006)* Career: *Valur Reykjavik, PSV, KR Reykjavik, Bolton W, Chelsea, Barcelona, Monaco, Tottenham Hotspur Stoke City (1995-2010).* Icelandic international striker, who was officially registered as a player with French side Monaco, but spent the second half of the 2009/10 season back in the capital, on loan to Tottenham Hotspur. Agreed a more permanent return to the Premiership in August 2010 when he signed a three year deal with Stoke City.

## GULLIT, Ruud

*Appearances: 64  Goals: 7 (1995-1998)*
*Career: Chelsea (1995-1998).* The Dutch
master was signed by Glenn Hoddle on a
free transfer from AC Milan to play as
sweeper. He immediately became a huge
hit with fans who recognised him as one of
the best all round players ever to have
played for the club. Was appointed player-
manager when Hoddle was head-hunted
by the FA to become the new England
boss. He brought silverware to the club in
the shape of the FA Cup in 1997, but was
sacked midway through the following
season, three months before the club won
the Cup Winners Cup.  Gullitt has since
managed Newcastle, Feyenoord and LA
Galaxy. Is now an ambassador for big
business and works as a television pundit.

## HALES, Kevin

*Appearances: 27  Goals: 2 (1979-1983)*
*Career: Chelsea. Leyton Orient. (1979-*
*1993).* Made his debut in 1979 but then
had to wait over a year until being
recalled to the side by John Neal for the
longest run of his Blues career. A string of
niggling injuries meant he could never
establish himself. Since hanging up his boots
he has worked for a number of non-league
clubs, most recently Rushden and Diamonds,
where he was assistant manager until June
2008. Having managed a cleaning firm, he is
now living on Merseyside, coaching and
scouting for Everton.

## HALL, Gareth

*Appearances: 171  Goals: 5 (1986-1996)*
*Career: Chelsea, Sunderland, Brentford,*
*Swinton Town. 1986-2001.* Was named
The Blues Young Player of the Year in 1985
and had captained both the youth and
reserve teams by the time he was 18.
Made his league debut in May 1987,
turning in the first of many trademark no
nonsense displays played at right back.
February 1990 saw him dislodge Steve
Clarke, but the arrival of Ian Porterfield as
manager in the summer of 1991 saw

Photo: Rod George

Clarke reinstalled with Hall requesting a
move. He stayed at Stamford Bridge for
another five years until the signing of Dan
Petrescu brought the curtain down on a
ten year Blues career. Hall is now a fully
qualified plasterer but has been the full
time assistant manager of Blue Square
Premier Hayes & Yeading United since
May 2007.  He had held the same job at
Yeading United before the clubs merged.

## HALSE, Harold

*Appearances: 111  Goals: 25 (1913-1921)*
*Career: Clapton Orient, Southend United,*
*Manchester United, Aston Villa, Chelsea,*
*Charlton Athletic. (1905-1923).* The first
player to play in three FA Cup finals for
different clubs, collecting a runners cup
medal with the Blues in 1915. Enjoyed his
best two seasons for the club, leading up
to World War 1. Ended his career with
Charlton and then scouted for them before
opening a tobacconists shop in Walton on
the Naze. Died in Colchester County
Hospital in March 1943 aged 63.

## HAMILTON, Ian

*Appearances: 5 Goals: 2 (1967-1968)*
*Career: Chelsea, Southend United, Aston Villa, Sheffield United. (1966-1977).* Is still in the record books as the youngest player ever to play a league game for the club. He made a goal scoring debut against Spurs in May 1967 aged only 16 years and 138 days. However, he was only at the club for another eight months before being sold to Southend for £5,000. Enjoyed success with Aston Villa and lived in the States for a number of years, where he coached at the Tommy Washington High School in Ohio. Upon his return to this country, he worked for the Nike organisation coaching soccer, and then as a play scheme organiser at Sheffield University.

## HAMPSHIRE, Steven

*Appearances: 1 Goals: 0 (1997-2000)*
*Career: Chelsea (1997-2000).* A Scottish born striker only made one appearance as sub for Ruud Gullit in a League Cup clash with Blackburn. Returned north of the Border and played for a decade. Now runs his own car valeting business.

## HAMPTON, Colin

*Appearances: 82 Goals: 0 (1914-1924)*
*Career: Chelsea, Crystal Palace. (1914-1926).* Spent the majority of his career at Stamford Bridge as understudy to Jim Molyneux. Won the military medal for gallantry during the World War One and then served as a special constable during the Second World War. Was awarded two benefit games for his long service with the club. Went onto run a confectionery shop in Brechin where he died in 1968.

## HANSON, Alf

*Appearances: 43 Goals: 9 (1938-1939)*
*Career: Liverpool, Chelsea. (1931-1939).* A fast and direct winger who cost £7,500, also played baseball for England. Was a plumber by trade, died in October 1993 aged 81.

Photo: l3nnon1975

## HARFORD, Mick

*Appearances: 34 Goals: 11 (1992-1993)*
*Career: Lincoln City, Newcastle United, Bristol City, Birmingham City, Luton Town, Derby County, Chelsea, Sunderland, Coventry City, Wimbledon. (1977-1998).* An old fashioned target man who was 33 years old when he was signed from newly relegated Luton Town for £300,000 and given his age it was never going to be a long stay. Despite being the club's top scorer, he was sold to Sunderland for £250,000 within a year. Has since worked in various capacities at Wimbledon, Luton, Nottingham Forest, Rotherham, Swindon, Colchester, Derby and most recently QPR until March 2010.

## HARLEY, Jon

*Appearances: 42 Goals: 2 (1997-2001)*
*Career: Chelsea, Wimbledon, Fulham, Sheffield United, West Ham United, Burnley, Watford, Notts County(1997-present day).* Came up through the ranks at Stamford Bridge, and made his league debut against Derby in 1998. Two years later was an unused sub in the FA Cup final victory but was unable to get a regular run of games thanks to the form of Celestine Babayaro and was sold to Fulham for £3.5m. Released by Watford in June 2010 and joined Notts County.

## HARMER, Tommy

*Appearances: 9  Goals: 1 (1962-1964)
Career: Tottenham Hotspur, Watford,
Chelsea. (1948-1964).* Was signed at the
age of 34 to help bring on the younger
players. Needed a cigarette before every
game to calm his nerves but was still a
quality performer despite the aging legs.
Scored a vital goal at Sunderland in the
1962-63 promotion winning season and
stayed on at the club as a youth coach
until 1967. Later worked as a warehouse
man in Hatton Garden and then as a
messenger for an Israeli bank in the West
End. Died in December 2007 aged 79.

## HARRIS, Allan

*Appearances 102  Goals: 1 (1960-1964
and 1966-1967)* Career: *Chelsea,
Coventry City, Chelsea, Queens Park
Rangers, Plymouth Argyle, Cambridge
United, (1960-1973).* Brother of Ron, was
twice an FA Youth Cup winner with the
Blues and was an unused sub in the 1967
FA Cup Final. He was assistant manager of
Barcelona and managed  Al-Ahly and
Malaysia until 2004. Has also worked as a
players agent, spending part the year in
the Far East.

*Photo: www.sporting-memorobilia.co.uk*

## HARRIS, John

*Appearances: 364  Goals: 14 (1945-1956)
Career: Swansea City, Tottenham
Hotspur, Wolverhampton Wanderers,
Chelsea, Chester City (1934-1959).* A
guest for the Blues during their two
Football League Cup South finals during
World War Two and signed on a
permanent basis for £8,000 as soon as
peace was announced. He gave the club
superb service which saw him part of the
1955 Championship winning team. Left for
Chester in 1956 were he became player
boss, then moved onto Sheffield United for
two spells in the hot seat on either side of
stints as general manager and chief scout.
Moved across the town to coach Sheffield
Wednesday before retiring. Later became
a lay preacher and died in Yorkshire in
July 1988 aged 71.

## HARRIS, Ron

*Appearances: 795  Goals: 14 (1961-1980)
Career: Chelsea, Brentford. (1961-1983).*
'Chopper' was a legendary Blues
hardman in the truest sense - he holds the
records for the most appearances and the
most number of league appearances for
the club. After being given his debut by
Tommy Docherty three months after
becoming an FA Youth Cup winner he was
an ever present in four of the seventeen
seasons he spent in the first team. As well
as playing in four major finals, in 1967 he
was the youngest player to lead a side out
for an FA Cup Final, and was undoubtedly
one of the sternest tests for any forward
during the sixties and seventies. Ron
brought Bramhill golf course in Wiltshire
for 400,000 and is reputed to have sold it
in 1989 for £2 million to Golf pro Roger
Mace and ex-Doncaster Rovers and
Aldershot Goalkeeper - Glen Johnson.
Then bought a holiday chalet and fishing
complex in a picturesque setting in a
village near Warminster, Wiltshire. Is now
in demand as a media pundit and after
dinner speaker.

# HARRIS, Charles

*Appearances: 2 Goals: 0 (1905-1909)*
*Career: Chelsea, Swansea City (1905-1910).* Played centre half in the Blues first ever league game at Stockport County. Was released to Swansea in 1909, where he spent over 30 years on the training staff until retiring. Died in London in 1967.

# HARRISON, Michael

*Appearances: 64 Goals: 9 (1957-1962)*
*Career: Chelsea, Blackburn Rovers, Plymouth Argyle, Luton Town. (1957-1970).* An extremely quick winger who had the misfortune to be around the club at the same time as Frank Blunstone. Made his league debut against Blackpool in April 1957 but had to spend almost the whole of the next six seasons in the reserves. Enjoyed his best season in 1961-62 when he appeared 22 times for the first team, scoring three goals. Was sold in September 1962 to Blackburn for £15,000. Worked as a Porter at Upney Hospital for a spell then moved back to Plymouth where he settled in Cremyll and worked as an insurance salesman.

# HARROW, Jack

*Appearances: 333 Goals: 5 (1911-1926)*
*Career: Chelsea (1911-1926).* Cost £50 from Croydon Common and went onto give 27 years service to the club. A strong defender, he was the first choice left back for almost eight seasons and was a member of the 1915 FA Cup losing side. Would have played even more games had it not been for the First World War. Helped the club to the 1919 London Victory Cup. Became a member of the training staff until retiring in 1938. Worked for Mitcham Council until 1956 but was dead two years later in July 1958

# HARWOOD, Jack

*Appearances: 4 Goals: 0 (1912-1913)*
*Career: Southend United, Chelsea, Portsmouth, Swansea Town,Aberdare*

*Athletic, Barrow (1910-1928).* Only played four games during his ten month stay at Stamford Bridge when Sam Downing was injured. Became trainer at Fulham and then Tooting and Mitcham until 1943. Died in London 13 years later.

Photo: hanszinsli

# HASSELBAINK, Jimmy Floyd

*Appearances: 177 Goals: 87 (2000-2004)*
*Career: Leeds United, Chelsea, Middlesbrough, Charlton Athletic, Cardiff City (1997-2008).* Arrived for a then club record £15 million and went onto give four years of fantastic service. He formed a deadly partnership with Eidur Gudjohnsen which produced 146 goals - Hasselbaink weighing in with 87 of them. He scored four in a game against Coventry City in 2001, ending the campaign as the Premier League's leading scorer and scorer of the first goal at Southampton's St Mary's Stadium. The goals dried up in his last two seasons and he was allowed to leave on a free transfer in 2004. Has started his UEFA A license and has worked for Sky as a pundit.

**GUESS WHO?** - see page 150 for answers. *Photo: Dan Davies*

## HATELEY, Tony

*Appearances: 33 Goals: 9 (1966-1967)*
*Career: Notts County, Aston Villa,*
*Chelsea, Liverpool, Coventry City,*
*Birmingham City, Notts County, Oldham*
*Athletic. (1958-1973).* Became the first
£100,000 signing in club history when
Tommy Docherty signed him from Aston
Villa to partner Tommy Baldwin after Peter
Osgood broke his leg. One of the best
headers of the ball in the game, he never
really justified his fee despite scoring the
winner against Leeds to book the Blues
first ever appearance in a Wembley Cup
Final. He was sold at the end of the season
to Liverpool with Chelsea getting their
money back. Upon retiring from the game,
set up his own business until 1978, when
he became Lottery Manager at Goodison
Park. Three years later became a drinks
rep before moving to the Preston area.
Was running a stall at Southport's indoor
market selling Christmas decorations.
Father of England striker Mark.

*Photo: Mattias Olsson*

## HAY, David

*Appearances: 120 Goals: 3 (1974-1980)*
*Career: Chelsea, (1974-1978).* The signing
of the Scottish international was supposed
to signal the start of a new era at Stamford
Bridge. An aggressive midfielder, he
moved south for £225,000 after falling out
with Celtic. His time in SW6 was hindered
by operations on his eyes and knees but
he did go on and become the cornerstone
of the 1976-77 promotion charge. Retired
through injury in 1979 and was appointed
assistant manager at Motherwell in the
November and Manager in September
1981. Managed his old club, Celtic then
became Chief Scout. Has twice managed
Livingstone as well as a stint at
Dunfermline. Now works in the media.

## HAZARD, Micky

*Appearances: 103 Goals: 12 (1985-1990)*
*Career: Tottenham Hotspur, Chelsea,*
*Portsmouth, Swindon Town, Tottenham*
*Hotspur. (1978-1995).* A creative
midfielder who was looking for a fresh
start when he was signed by John Hollins
for £310,000. He never really established
himself in four and a half years at the club
due to injury, illness and disputes with
managers. Was sold to Portsmouth for
£100,000. Has worked as a youth coach
for Spurs and Crystal Palace but is now
working as a black cab driver in London.

## HEDMAN, Magnus

*Appearances 0 Goals 0 (2006-2007)*
*Career: Coventry City, Chelsea. (1997-*
*2007).* Had officially retired from football
when he made a sensational comeback to
help out during an injury crisis. He never
made a first team appearance despite
being handed the 22 squad number. Later
worked as a television pundit in Sweden
and Spain but was convicted of using
banned steroids by a Stockholm court and
was sacked by the television company. His
business hit the rocks and he now claims
that he has spent the estimated £10
million earned from his career.

## HENDERSON, Stewart

*Appearances: 0 Goals: 0 (1964)*
Career: *Chelsea, Brighton, Reading (1964-1982).* Former full back, joined the ground staff as a 17 year-old but never made the grade and was allowed to join Brighton on a free transfer. Stayed on at his last club,Reading, as coach, scout and spongeman. He later moved to Southampton as youth development officer and is now reserve team manager.

## HEWITT, Tom

*Appearances: 8 Goals: 0 (1911-1913)*
Career: *Wrexham, Chelsea, Swansea Town. (1910-1920).* Joined the Blues for £350 but found his chances at full back limited because of competition from Water Betteridge and John Cameron. He had his fair share of injuries in his two seasons at the club which didn't help his quest for regular football either. An engineer by trade, Hewitt became a commercial traveller later in life but died in December 1980 aged 90.

## HILSDON, George

*Appearances: 164 Goals: 107 (1906-1912)* Career: *West Ham United, Chelsea, West Ham United, Gillingham. (1903-1923).* Was said to have been London's first football star, scored five goals on is debut against Glossop North End, and his 27 goals in his first season helped the club win promotion to the First Division. Scored six goals in the Blues record 9-1 FA Cup victory against Worksop Town. His legend lived on at the club for many years following his departure, a statuette of a footballer modelled on him decorated a weather vane on the roof of a stand at the North End of Stamford Bridge. Joined Fred Karno's troop in 1924, later he lived in East Ham and scraped a living. Died in Leicester in 1941 following his evacuation from the capital. His funeral was attended by only four people and no stone marks his grave in Wigston cemetery, Leicester.

## HINSHELWOOD, Wally

*Appearances: 14 Goals: 1 (1951)*
Career: *Fulham, Chelsea, Fulham, Reading, Bristol City, Millwall, Newport County. (1946-1961).* Spent 15 weeks at the club following a swap deal involving Jim Bowie when the outside right position was giving cause for concern. He quickly returned to Craven Cottage for a fee of £3,000. Spent 26 years as a caretaker in New Addington. Now lives in retirement in Selsey. The father of Martin, who had a spell as Chelsea's reserve coach in 1985.

## HINTON, Marvin

*Appearances: 344 Goals: 4 (1963-1976)*
Career: *Charlton Athletic, Chelsea, Barnet (1957-1976).* An outstanding football brain, Hinton was signed for £30,000 and could play at full back and in central defence, where he was dominating and rarely embarrassed. He was part of Sir Alf Ramsey's original 40 man World Cup squad but didn't make the final cut, however he did win League Cup and FA Cup winners medals. The arrival of David Webb in 1967 was supposed to signal the end of his stay in SW6 but he hung around for another nine years taking his service to 13 seasons. Was running his own Office removals business until he was involved in car crash near his home in Crawley, Sussex.

## HITCHCOCK, Kevin

*Appearances: 135 (1988-1999)*
Career: *Nottingham Forest, Mansfield Town, Chelsea, Northampton Town. (1983-1999).* Became Bobby Campbell's first signing for the club when he was signed for £250,000. Spent a total of 11 years at the club and was virtually second choice keeper for the whole of that time. He still won FA Cup, League Cup and Cup Winners' Cup winners medals. Became a goalkeeping coach with Watford before linking up with former Chelsea team mate Mark Hughes at Blackburn, Manchester City and since August 2010, Fulham.

## HODDINOTT, Frank

*Appearances: 32 Goals: 4 (1921-1923)*
Career: *Watford, Chelsea, Crystal Palace.*
*(1919-1926).* The inside forward cost
£3,500 but never lived up to his reputation
as a goalscorer. Was mainly played out of
position, at centre forward, because of an
injury to Jack Cook. Worked on pleasure
boats in Southend for many years and
died in the town in 1980 aged 86.

*Photo: Badger Swan*

## HODDLE, Glenn

*Appearances: 39 Goals: 1 (1993-1995)*
Career: *Tottenham Hotspur, Swindon
Town, Chelsea (1975-1995).* Hoddle's
appointment as Chelsea's player-boss in
1993 was supposed to mark a new era in
club history. He had a non contract spell at
the club playing for the reserves in 1991
and although he had seen better days as
a player, he still displayed some of the
skills which made him one of the most
gifted players in English football history.
He employed a 3-5-2 system, which had
served him well at Swindon Town, playing
himself as the spare defender. The club
qualified for Europe in all of his seasons in
charge and had reached the 1994 FA Cup
Final by the time he was head-hunted by
The FA to over as boss of the national
team. Had a three year spell in charge of
England which ended controversially after
comment about disabled people in a
newspaper interview.

He has also managed Swindon Town,
Southampton, Tottenham Hotspur and
Wolverhampton Wanderers. He now runs
his own Soccer Academy in Jerez, Spain.

## HOGH, Jes

*Appearances: 17 Goals: 0 (1999-2001)*
Career: *Chelsea (1999-2001).* A £300,000
signing from Turkish side Fenerbahce but
found competition tough from Marcel
Desailly, Frank Leboeuf and Mario
Melchiot, and then suffered a serious
ankle injury which forced him into an
early retirement. Suffered a stroke in a
Copenhagen hotel room in 2007 and as a
result he has suffered some serious health
problems which caused him to lose his
job and wife.

## HOLLINS, John

*Appearances: 592 Goals: 64 (1963-1975
and 1983-1984)* Career: *Chelsea, Queens
Park Rangers, Arsenal, Chelsea. (1963-
1983).* Made his debut as a 17 year-old
and, from the start of the 1964-65 season,
made the number four shirt almost
exclusively his own for the next decade.
He played in two League Cup Finals, two
FA Cup Finals and a Cup Winners' Cup
final, only missing the replay against Real
Madrid due to an injury. He followed Dave
Sexton to QPR for £80,000 in June 1975,
but returned to the Bridge eight years
later on a free transfer from Arsenal to
help win promotion back to the First
Division. Joined the coaching staff and
succeeded John Neal as manager. Won
the Full Members cup but was sacked in
March 1988 following a run of poor
results. After leaving Chelsea, he became
a financial adviser before returning to the
game as Reserve Team Coach at Queens
Park Rangers, has also had spells at
Swansea, Rochdale, Stockport, Crawley
Town and Weymouth now works as an
advisor to football clubs, can be seen on
TV and has a suite named after him at
Stamford Bridge. His son Chris is now a
well known face on BBCtv.

## HOLTON, Pat

*Appearances: 1 Goals: 0 (1959-1960)
Career: Chelsea, Southend United (1959-1961).* Signed for £6,000 from Scottish club Motherwell but never settled. Only played one game and was allowed to join Southend. Soon returned to Scotland where he coached junior football in the Hamilton area. Worked for the water board and still lives in the area in retirement.

## HOPE, James

*Appearances: 1 Goals: 0 (1930-1932)
Career: Gateshead, Chelsea. (1928-1932).* A reserve team regular for 18 months but only played one first team game - replacing Willie Ferguson at left half in a 2-1 home defeat against Blackburn Rovers. Returned to Scotland where he lived and worked in Dunfermline before his death in 1977.

## HOPKIN, David

*Appearances: 46 Goals: 1 (1992-1995)
Career: Chelsea. Crystal Palace, Leeds United, Bradford City, Crystal Palace. (1992-2002).* When he arrived at the club for £300,000 from Morton it was as a right winger, but when Glenn Hoddle took over at the club he was forced to re-invent himself in a more central midfield role. He still didn't ever really establish himself in the first team despite his hard working ethic and never looked comfortable away from the touchline. Was sold to Crystal Palace for £850,000 in 1995, where he made his name. Later settled in Scotland and worked at the Port of Glasgow. Now lives in Greenock, where he runs a newsagent's shop.

## HOUSEMAN, Peter

*Appearances: 343 Goals: 39 (1962-1975)
Career: Chelsea, Oxford United. (1962-1977).* Took his time to convince not only Tommy Docherty but also a sceptical Blues faithful of his ability. It was four years before he finally established himself in the first team.

He provided the ammo for Ian Hutchinson and Peter Osgood and played a vital role in the 1970 Cup run, scoring a critical goal in the replay at Burnley, and then the equaliser against Leeds in the Wembley Final. He was an ever present in the Cup Winners' Cup winning side and stayed at Stamford Bridge until the club were relegated in 1975. The winger was killed in a car crash near Oxford in March 1977, aged 31, when returning home with his wife, hours after he had played in a game. He had also set up and coached a youth team in Oakley, Hampshire

## HOUSTON, Stewart

*Appearances: 14 Goals: 0 (1962-1972)
Career: Chelsea, Brentford, Manchester United, Sheffield United, Colchester United. (1967-1985).* Bought to the club from his native Scotland by Tommy Docherty. Only made 14 appearances in his five years in SW6 because of the amount of time that he spent on the treatment table and it was only when he left that club for Brentford that he developed into a quality left back. Has twice been caretaker manager of Arsenal, taken control of QPR where he also scouted and coached a number of other clubs. He is now scouting for the Gunners.

## HOWARD, Terry

*Appearances: 6 Goals: 0 (1984-1987)
Career: Chelsea, Crystal Palace, Chester City, Leyton Orient, Wycombe Wanderers. (1984-1996).* A versatile former England youth international who was a mainstay of the reserve team for three seasons. He was a regular goal scorer but found first team chances hard to come and even then, filling in for either Joey Jones or Darren Wood at right back. Probably best remember for being sacked by manager John Sitton at half time in a match for Leyton Orient against Blackpool which was featured on a television documentary Orient – Club for a fiver. Now lives in Romford and works in Billingsgate Fish Market.

## HOWARTH, Jack

*Appearances: 0  Goals: 0 (1963-1964)
Career: Chelsea, Swindon Town,
Aldershot, Rochdale, Aldershot,
Bournemouth, Southport. (1963-1978).*
Signed by the Blues from a local team,
Stanley United, in his native North East but
was allowed to leave the club without
making a first team appearance just 12
months later. Is now working for the Post
Office in Romsey, Hampshire.

Photo: Phil Calvert

## HUDSON, Alan

*Appearances: 189  Goals: 14 (1968-1974
and 1983-1984) Career: Chelsea, Stoke
City, Arsenal, Chelsea, Stoke City. (1968-
1985).* Alan Hudson will be remembered
as one of the most flamboyant players
ever to have played for the club. Born just
a stone's throw away from the Kings Road,
he rejected his boyhood club Fulham to
sign for Chelsea. A bone infection lost him
the tag as the youngest ever debutant for
the club, instead he had to wait nine
months to make his first team bow. Soon
established himself as the team's
playmaker, creating goals for Peter
Osgood and Ian Hutchinson and he
played a key role in the successful Cup
Winners' Cup campaign after missing out
on the FA Cup final against Leeds United
twelve months earlier through injury. His
first spell at the club ended at the age age
of just 22, when he fell out with Dave

Sexton and was sold to Stoke City for
£240,000. He returned to Stamford Bridge
nine years later but never played a game
because of injury and illness. Scored a
'goal that never was' in his first spell
against Ipswich Town in 1970. After
shooting into the side netting, referee Roy
Capley signalled a goal. Alan later settled
in the Potteries where he had business
interests and wrote for the local paper
before suffering alcoholism and
bankruptcy. Spent two months in a coma
after being knocked down by a car in East
London in December 1997 but has made
a full recovery. Is now an occasional
author and pundit.

## HUGHES, Billy

*Appearances: 105  Goals: 0 (1948-1951)
Career: Swansea Town, Birmingham City,
Luton Town, Chelsea, Hereford United.
(1935-1954).* Welsh international full back
who had celebrated his 30th birthday
when he arrived from Luton Town for
£12,000 after World War Two. He had
never settled at Kenilworth Road but
quickly found his feet in London. A good
tackler and distributor of the ball, he gave
four years excellent service to the club.
Became landlord of the Bluebell Inn,
Halkyn after retiring. Then scouted for
Chester City but returned to the Midlands
in 1969 to work as steward at the Wolesley
Car Social Club. Died in Birmingham in
June 1981 aged 63.

## HUGHES, Harry

*Appearances: 1  Goals: 0 (1951-1952)
Career: Southport, Chelsea,
Bournemouth, Gillingham. (1950-1962)..*
Played his only senior game against
Liverpool in August 1951 replacing John
Saunders. Unfortunately he soon had John
Harris blocking his path to the first team
and after 16 months at the club was sold
to Bournemouth for £1,500. Ran the Club
shop at Spurs for eleven years, before
moving to Guildford where he was self
employed.

Photo: Kate Boydell

# HUGHES, Mark

*Appearances: 123  Goals: 39 (1995-1998)*
Career: *Manchester United, Chelsea, Southampton, Everton, Blackburn Rovers. (1980-2002).* Welsh international 'Sparky' had spells abroad with Barcelona and Bayern Munich before arriving at the Bridge in a £1.5 million deal just two years after scoring against the Blues in the FA Cup Final. Was a key player in the club's resurgence, forming a formidable partnership with Giafranco Zola. One of the best attackers in the game, he added an FA Cup winner's medal to his collection in 1997 and then helped the club to League Cup and Cup Winners' Cup success. Just 12 months later he was sold on to Southampton. Went into management with Wales, Blackburn and Manchester City until December 2009. In August 2010 he was appointed manager of Fulham.

# HUGHES, Paul

*Appearances: 23  Goals: 2 (1994-2000)*
Career: *Chelsea, Stockport County, Norwich City, Crewe Alexandra, Southampton, Luton Town. (1994-2006).* Scored an impressive solo effort on his debut against Derby County, but over the next three years injuries and Gianluca Vialli's policy of big name foreign signings like Roberto Di Matteo, Gus Poyet and Didier Deschamps hardly allowed him a

look in. He was a member of the 1998 FA Cup and Cup Winners' Cup squads however, was eventually released on a free transfer. Was then signed by Glenn Hoddle who was by then Southampton boss. Helped form a company that provides park teams with websites. Has also coached at Brunel University but is now reserve team coach at Hayes and Yeading.

# HUGHES, Tommy

*Appearances: 11  Goals: 0 (1965-1971)*
Career: *Chelsea, Aston Villa, Brighton & Hove Albion, Hereford United. (1965-1982).* A Scottish under-23 international who arrived from Clydebank. As understudy to Peter Bonetti, he found first team opportunities few and far between and was forced to leave Stamford Bridge to seek regular football. Suffered a broken leg and John Phillips was signed from Aston Villa and when he recovered he was sold to Villa for £12,500 to replace his replacement. Had a short spell as Hereford boss but settled in the town where he owns a carpet cleaning business.

# HUMPHREYS, Percy

*Appearances: 46  Goals: 13 (1908-1909)*
Career: *Queens Park Rangers, Notts County, Leicester Fosse, Chelsea, Tottenham Hotspur, Leicester Fosse, Hartlepool United, Norwich City. (1900-1914).* A strong inside forward who was signed for £350 but left the club almost as soon as Vivian Woodward joined in December 1909 and signed for Spurs. He also had the last laugh by scoring the goal that relegated his former employers on the last day of the same season. Managed Hartlepool and then Swiss side FC Basel but he was forced to return home just months after signing a three year deal after the outbreak of World War One. Became a car checker, and lived in retirement in Stepney, East London, until he killed himself in April 1959 aged 78.

## HUNTER, George

*Appearances: 32 Goals: 2 (1913-1914)*
*Career: Aston Villa. Oldham Athletic.*
*Chelsea, Manchester United, Portsmouth.*
*(1908-1922).* A fiery wing half nicknamed
'Cocky' suffered from discipline problems.
He only spent one season at Stamford
Bridge after a £1,000 arrival because it is
said that his manager at the time, David
Calderhead, nor his team mates could
control him. In the end the the club made
a £300 profit on the deal when he was
sold to Manchester United. Wrote a light
hearted football book before going onto
serve as a sergeant-major in the army
during the World War One. Saw action in
France and Gallipoli, but then served
three months hard labour in August 1930
for deserting his wife and children. Died
in February 1934 aged 46.

## HUTCHINGS, Chris

*Appearances: 101 Goals: 3 (1980-1983)*
*Career: Chelsea, Brighton & Hove Albion,*
*Huddersfield Town, Walsall, Rotherham*
*United. (1980-1994).* Chris was plucked
out of non league football by Geoff Hurst
when he paid Harrow Borough £5,000 to
secure the services of the former
Southend trainee. He won plenty of friends
during his three and a half years at
Stamford Bridge for his desire to get
forward. He left for Brighton three months
after being find £250 for using insulting
words to a policeman following a game
between the two clubs. Went into
management and has taken charge of
Bradford City and Wigan Athletic in the
Premier League, had a spell as caretaker
Derby boss. Since January 2009, has been
in charge of one of his former clubs
Walsall.

## HUTCHINSON, Ian

*Appearances: 144 Goals: 58 (1968-1976)*
*Career: Chelsea, (1968-1975).*
Remembered for his famous long throw
ins, he was signed from Cambridge
United after Frank Blunstone was asked to
go and watch a goalkeeper. Hutch caught

his eye and Dave Sexton and coach Ron
Suart were soon dispatched to watch him.
He then had to interrupt his honeymoon to
sign the deal after a £5,000 bid was
accepted. He provided the ideal foil for
Peter Osgood, powerful in the air, he
headed the second equaliser in the 1970
FA Cup Final against Leeds. Then in the
replay, his missile like throw was headed
in by Dave Webb for the winner. His
career never hit the heights it threatened
because of injuries. During his time at the
club he suffered two broken legs, a badly
broken ankle, a dislocated knee, problem
toe as well as almost persistent knee
injuries. He kept on making returns until
July 1976 when he retired aged 27 and
worked in Chelsea's commercial
department. A qualified Cordon Bleu chef,
he helped out with the catering at
Brentford FC and ran a pub in Windsor
with his old team-mate Peter Osgood.
Later worked in corporate hospitality for
several clubs and as a curator at a London
art gallery before his death in September
2002 after a long illness.

Photo: Spree Pix

## HUTH, Robert

*Appearances: 42 Goals: 0 (2002-2006)*
*Career: Chelsea, Middlesbrough, Stoke*
*City (2002-2010.* Joined his current club,
Stoke City for £5 million in August 2009.

# HUXFORD, Cliff

*Appearances: 7 Goals: 0 (1955-1959)*
Career: *Chelsea, Southampton, Exeter City. (1958-1967).* A tough tackler who impressed in the reserves but could never properly establish himself in the first team. Lives outside Southampton and worked as a painter and decorator, also managed a number of non league teams.

# ILES, Bob

*Appearances: 14 Goals: 0 (1978-1983)*
Career: *Bournemouth, Chelsea. (1973-1983).* Spent five years at the club after a £10,000 move from non-league Weymouth, and was deputy to four different keepers. A decent shot stopper with good hands, he never got the first team run that over 100 appearances for the reserves deserved. Was released and joined Wealdstone where he played at Wembley alongside Stuart Pearce and Vinnie Jones. Now lives back in Dorset where he works as an agent for international yacht brokers. Is a member of Dorset Sailing Club, where he races with his wife. Since retiring from football he has established himself as an accomplished sailor, winning races at a national level.

# IRVING, Sam

*Appearances: 97 Goals: 5 (1928-1932)*
Career: *Bristol City, Cardiff City, Chelsea, Bristol Rovers. (1913-1933).* Played for Cardiff in their FA Cup Final win over Arsenal and arrived at Stamford Bridge well into his 30's but it didn't stop him from playing a key role in the 1929-30 promotion winning campaign. Toured South America with the club and when the players had oranges thrown at them, his response was to pick one up, peel it and eat it. Was released by The Blues after his 38th birthday. Despite hailing from Belfast he returned to Dundee where he had two spells as a player and opened a billiard hall. Was involved in a takeover of Dundee United, where he had a spell as manager and director. He remained in the area until his death in December 1968 aged 75.

# ISAAC, Robert

*Appearances: 13 Goals: 0 (1983-1987)*
Career: *Chelsea, Brighton. (1984-1988).* Was the rising star of the youth and reserve teams and impressed enough to be named Young Player of the Year in 1984. Could play either in central defence or full back and made his league debut replacing Colin Pates at Watford. With more established players ahead of him in the pecking order, he was sold to Brighton for £35,000 in February 1987. A knee injury forced his retirement and he became a personal assistant for a well known racing family.

# ISSA, Pierre

*(2001)*
Career: *Chelsea, Watford. (2001-2002).* The South African international joined the Blues on loan from Marseille, but never played a first team game and the deal never became permanent. Is best remembered for falling off a stretcher while at Watford in a game against Birmingham. Carried on playing abroad until 2009 with OFI in Crete. Is now a players agent based in Beirut, Lebanon.

# JACKSON, Alex

*Appearances: 77 Goals: 29 (1930-1932)*
Career: *Huddersfield Town, Chelsea. (1925-1933).* The 'Flying Scotsman' was a major box office attraction when he became the first of a string of big name signings who were supposed to lead the charge for honours. He arrived for £8,500 from Huddersfield Town and his debut against Sheffield Wednesday attracted a crowd of 51,000. A difference of opinion with the club's management saw him walk out on the club two years later. After playing non-league soccer both here and in France, he quit playing at the age of 28. Having joined the army and rising to the rank of major, he was killed in a car crash while serving in Cairo in November 1946.

## JACKSON, John

*Appearances: 51 Goals: 0 (1933-1945)*
Career: *Chelsea. (1933-1945).* One of the
best goalkeepers in the country in his day
and was said to be as 'brave as a Lion'.
Found his way to regular first team football
blocked by the great Vic Woodley.
Started the 1934-35 season as first choice
until picking up a nasty injury which let
the England star back in. Emigrated to
Canada after the war and became a
professional golfer, returning to the UK in
1950 to play the British Open, died in
Nova Scotia in June 1965 aged 59.

## JAROSIK, Jiri

*Appearances: 14 Goals: 0 (2005-2006)*
Career: *Sparta Prague, CSKA Moscow,
Chelsea, (Birmingham City (loan), Celtic,
Krylia Sovetov, Zaragoza (1996 -2010).* A
Czech international who was brought into
the club in January 2005 from CSKA
Moscow. However, the arrival of Michael
Essien seven months later restricted his
first team appearances. He was sent out
on loan to Birmingham City, before being
sold to Celtic the following June.
After a spell in Russia with Krylia Sovetov,
Jarosik signed for Real Zaragoza in Spain
on 14th January 2010.

## JASPER, Dale

*Appearances: 15 Goals: 0 (1982-1986)*
Career: *Chelsea, Brighton & Hove Albion,
Crewe Alexandra. (1982-1991).* A classy
player on his day who skippered the
reserves to the Football Combination
League title in 1985. Only made 15 first
team appearances due to a string of
injuries, including a foot injury after he
had finally managed to dislodge John
Bumstead from the side. Jasper is now
living in South London and is working in
the building industry.

## JENKINS, Thomas

*Appearances: 5 Goals: 0 (1949-1951)*
Career: *Chelsea. (1949-1951).* Arrived
from Scottish outfit Queen of the South in
July 1949 for £8,000 with a big reputation.
Sadly, he never lived up to the tag and
spent almost the whole of his two years at
the club playing in the reserves. Moved to
Sunderland in 1951, a return to the club
that he had played for during the war. He
also worked for Rolls Royce, becoming
Chief Draughtsman by the time of his
retirement. Jenkins maintained his fitness
by playing badminton and squash well
into 70's and was also an Aikido instructor,
black belt 3rd dan. Locally he was the star
player in the local pub quiz team. He died
in May 2008 following a stroke aged 83.

## JOHNSEN, Erland

*Appearances: 183  Goals: 1 (1989-1997)*
Career: *Chelsea (1989-1997)*. A tough, uncompromising, hard tackling centre half, arrived in November 1989 in a £306,000 deal from Bayern Munich. Soon formed a decent partnership with Ken Monkou. Although popular with the fans, he found himself out of favour for almost two and a half seasons until David Webb was appointed manager and restored him to the first team. He continued to go from strength to strength and won the Player of the Year award in 1996, but within 12 months had decided to go home to Norway. He has since managed a number of clubs and is currently player developer at Lillestrom SK.

## JOHNSON, Glenn

*Appearances: 41  Goals: 3 (2003-2007)*
Career: *West Ham United, Millwall (loan), Chelsea, Portsmouth, Liverpool (2002-2010*. Became the first purchase of the Abramovich era  when he was snapped up from West Ham for about £6 million, following their relegation from the premiership. Was sold to Portsmouth in 2007 but remarkably, Johnson almost re-joined the Blues in June 2009 when the south coast club were keen to ease their financial troubles. Although a bid from the club had been accepted by Portsmouth, the player decided to join Liverpool in an £17 million deal.

## JOHNSTONE, Derek

*Appearances: 4  Goals: 0 (1983-1985)*
Career: *Rangers, Chelsea Dundee United, Rangers (1968-1986)*. Was almost 30 when he arrived at Stamford Bridge for £30,000 to add competition for places with Kerry Dixon and David Speedie. Part of a clear out by Rangers boss John Greig, he never really settled in West London. Had a spell on loan at Dundee United before going back to Ibrox 18 months after his departure, for £25,000. A legend north of the border, he has carved out a career in the media mainly for BBC Scotland and Radio Clyde.

## JOKANOVIC, Slavisa

*Appearances: 53  Goals: 0 (2000-2002)*
Career: *Chelsea 2000-2002*. A Serbian international who was signed by Claudio Ranieri for £1.7 million from Deportivo La Coruna to replace the injured Roberto Di Matteo. Never really enjoyed a settled run in the team because of a rotation policy in his two years at the club. Moved to Madrid and joined the technical staff of third division Club Atletico de Pisto before returning to his former club Partizan. As head coach he led them to a league and cup double but resigned in September 2009 citing a feud within the club's board as the reason for his departure.

## JONES, Evan

*Appearances: 21  Goals: 4 (1909-1911)*
Career: *Chelsea, Oldham Athletic, Bolton Wanderers, Swansea Town. (1909-1920)*. Cost £300 from Welsh side Aberdare to understudy George Hilsdon but didn't take long to force his way into the first team after scoring a hat trick on his debut. After that found it hard to get a regular game at Stamford Bridge and was sold at a £100 profit to Oldham where he enjoyed more success. Became a coal miner until breaking his leg in an accident. Then worked for a maritime washery and ended his working life with the Western Bus Company.

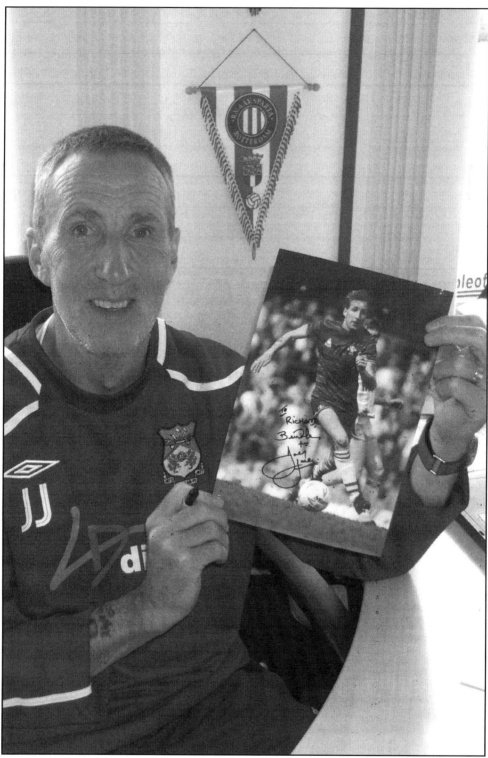

**Joey Jones**. *Photo: Retro Reds*

## JONES, Joey

*Appearances: 91 Goals: 2 (1982-1985)*
Career: *Wrexham, Liverpool, Wrexham, Chelsea, Huddersfield Town, Wrexham. (1972-1991).* Joined a struggling Chelsea team for £34,500 and helped restore morale with his performances on the pitch and his dressing room banter. Became a crowd favourite after an initial bad start when he was sent off on his debut at Carlisle. A close pal of Mickey Thomas, he spent much of his time in SW6 living in Wrexham but he was still able to play a vital role in the club's march to the Second Division title in 1984. His reluctance to relocate to the capital and absence from training saw John Hollins bring in Doug Rougvie. Jones was relegated to the role of understudy but still managed to play 21 games as a utility man. Hung around at the club for another year but was sold for £35,000 to Huddersfield in 1985. A Wrexham legend, has coached the reserves, youth team and is now first team coach.

## JONES, Keith

*Appearances: 69 Goals: 10 (1983-1987)*
Career: *Chelsea, Brentford, Southend United, Colchester United, Charlton Athletic, Reading. (1983-2002).* Made his league debut against Barnsley in March 1983 and after scoring four goals in his first ten games it appeared that he was set for a long run in the first team. A drubbing at the hands of Man Utd resulted in him being taken off at half time and resulted in him spending the next 18 months only making the occasional first team appearance. A make or break run in the 1986-97 saw him fail to recreate his initial promise and he was later sold to Brentford for £40,000, where his career soon picked up again. Became a personal soccer trainer after hanging up his boots while coaching part time at Tooting and Mitcham. Then landed a job in the US, coaching at Charlton's US Academy. Also helped out with Coweta Cannons and Atlanta Silverbacks women's team. Is now in Phoenix, Arizona coaching FC Sol.

*Photo: Byron and Tamara*

## JONES, Vinnie

*Appearances: 52 Goals: 7 (1991-1992)*
Career: *Wimbledon, Leeds United, Sheffield United, Chelsea, Wimbledon, QPR. (1986-1997).* One of the game's modern day 'hard men' who gave everything for the cause during his time on the pitch. Was signed by Ian Porterfield as a key part of his rebuilding plans which allowed Andy Townsend to get further forward. Always a target for referees, which meant that he missed the Blues' FA Cup quarter final against Sunderland which ended in defeat. His crowning moment came when crashing home a 25-yard stunner to help earn a win against Liverpool at Anfield. In 1992, he found himself shipped out of the club when Porterfield turned to Nigel Spackman to perform his midfield role. 13 months after arriving, he was sold to Wimbledon for £700,000, generating a £125,000 profit. Worked as a hod carrier before turning pro and has since become a popular Hollywood film star! Now splits his time between Los Angeles and Hertfordshire. In one of many TV appearances, he took part in Celebrity Big Brother in 2010.

## JUDGE, Alan

*Appearances:0 Goals: 0 (1984)*
*Career: Luton Town, Reading, Oxford
United, Lincoln City, Cardiff City,
Hereford United, Chelsea, Swindon Town,
Oxford United. (1979-2004).* Was signed
as goalkeeping cover for the Cup
Winners' Cup but was never called into
action and left again without playing a
game for the club. Survived bowel cancer
and now works as a goalkeeping coach
and a driving instructor.

## KEENAN, Joe

*Appearances: 3 Goals:0 (1999-2006)*
*Career: Chelsea, Brentford. (1999-2006).*
Made his first team debut as a substitute
for John Terry and was later earmarked as
one for the future by Claudio Ranieri. He
labelled him as a hot prospect and gave
him a four year contract. Unfortunately,
Keenan broke his leg soon afterwards and
only made one further appearance under
Jose Mourinho before being given a free
transfer. Has played in Holland, Belgium
and Scotland and is now in a second spell
in Australia playing for South Melbourne
in the Victoria Premier League.

## KELL, Len

*Appearances: 3 Goals: 0 (1952-1954)*
*Career: Chelsea, Norwich City. (1952-
1955).* Spent four years on the ground staff
before making his league debut in a win
against Arsenal at Highbury in November
1953. Is likely to have played more had it
not been for his two years of national
service but with stiff competition for
places from Johnny McNichol and Les
Stubbs, he was allowed to join Norwich
City in 1954. After a spell playing and
coaching in Australia, he to returned to his
trade as a painter and decorator. He set
up his own successful business, which he
combined with running a hotel in Great
Yarmouth. Now living in retirement on the
East Coast, Len was also a successful
breeder of Staffordshire Bull Terriers and
was a seven time champion at Crufts.

## KEMBER, Steve

*Appearances: 150 Goals: 15 (1971-1975)*
*Career: Crystal Palace, Chelsea,
Leicester City, Crystal Palace. (1965-
1979).* Was Chelsea's was expensive
player at the time when Dave Sexton
splashed out £170,000. Crystal Palace, the
club he had been at since the age of five,
needed the cash. He rarely produced his
best form for Chelsea after being asked
to play on the right rather than in his
preferred role of through the middle. Was
moved into the heart of the action towards
the end of his stay, but was sold to
Leicester City when the club were forced
to sell off players. Owned a Wine Bar in
Croydon, was on the coaching staff at
Palace, including a four stint in the
manager's hot seat. Now a coach at
Whitgift School and scouts for Fulham.

## KENNEDY, George

*Appearances: 12 Goals: 0 (1908-1909)*
*Career: Lincoln City, Chelsea, Brentford
(1906-1913).* A half back who followed
manager David Calderhead to Stamford
Bridge. Only spent one season with the
club before leaving for Brentford. Was
killed in the battle for Passchendaele in
December 1917.

## KEVAN, Derek

*Appearances: 7 Goals: 1 (1963)*
*Career: Bradford Park Avenue, West
Bromwich Albion, Chelsea, Manchester
City, Crystal Palace, Peterborough, Luton
Town, Stockport County. (1952-1967).* An
England international nicknamed the
'Tank' was bought to London by Tommy
Docherty for £50,000 in March 1963. His
only goal for the club was in the 7-0 rout
over Portsmouth which clinched
promotion. The strict discipline and
demanding training methods of the
manager led to a fall out between the pair
and he was sold to Man City for £35,000.
Is now retired living in Castle Vale,
Birmingham after working in a pub, as a
delivery driver and for a Sign Company.

## KEZMAN, Mateja

*Appearances: 41 Goals: 7 (2004-2005)*
Career: *Chelsea (2004-2005).* The
Serbian international hit man was signed
for £5.2 million in the summer of 2004 to
bolster the Blues front line, but despite
making his debut on the opening day of
the season he had to wait until December
for his first goal. Went onto score the
winning goal in the Carling Cup Final
victory over Liverpool and helped the
club to their first League title in 50 years.
Left after only one season having failed to
settle in London. Has played for Atletico
Madrid, Fenerbahce, and currently Paris
St Germain, but had an unsuccessful loan
spell at Zenit St Petersburg.

## KHARINE, Dmitri

*Appearances: 146 Goals: 0 (1992-1999)*
Career: *Chelsea. (1992-1999).* A Moscow
native, he spent a decade playing for
three clubs in the city before joining The
Blues in December 1992 for £400,000.
Impressed in the run to the 1994 FA Cup
Final but suffered injuries towards the
latter part of his stay at the club. Ended his
professional career in Scotland at Celtic
and finally hung up his gloves after a spell
with Hornchurch. Has been goalkeeping
coach at Luton Town since 2004.

## KIRKUP, Joe

*Appearances: 69 Goals: 2 (1966-1968)*
Career: *West Ham United, Chelsea,
Southampton. (1958-1973).* The former
England Under 23 international was a
cultured player who was bought to add
some maturity to defence. He was a
substitute in the 1967 FA Cup Final but
largely remained out of favour until Dave
Sexton replaced Tommy Docherty as
manager. Ran a pub in Alton, then owned
Sports shop in Cranleigh before opening
his own newsagents in Ewell, Surrey. Has
now retired to the South of France.

*Photo: Thanks to Christine Matthews*

## KIRWAN, Jack

*Appearances: 76 Goals: 18 (1905-1908)*
Career: *Everton, Tottenham Hotspur,
Chelsea, Leyton Orient. (1898-1910).* The
outside left joined the newly formed
Chelsea for their first two seasons in the
Football League and quickly became a
crowd favourite. Forming an excellent left
wing partnership with Jimmy Windridge,
he only missed two games in the clubs
first season and only three in their second
campaign. Also won four Ireland caps
while at the club. Kept his most prized
possession, the ball from the 1901 FA Cup
Final, with him until his death in Hendon,
London, in January 1959 aged 80. He had
settled back in London after becoming
Ajax's first ever manager and coaching
Livorno in Italy. Before taking up football
he won a Gaelic All Ireland Championship
with Dublin.

## KITAMIRIKE, Joel

*Appearances: 1 Goals: 0 (2001-2004)*
Career: *Chelsea, Brentford, Aldershot,
(2001-2005).* His only senior appearance
came alongside John Terry in a UEFA Cup
clash with Hapoel Tel Aviv. Then spent a
season on loan at Brentford before being
released. Drifted into non-league football
but was sentenced to 20 months in prison
in November 2008 for supplying Class A
drugs.

## KITCHENER, Ray

*Appearances: 1 Goals: 0 (1954-1956)*
Career: *Chelsea, Norwich City. (1954-
1957).* A reserve team regular in his two
seasons at Stamford Bridge, played one
league game against Manchester City at
Main Road and several friendly games but
competition from England international
Frank Blunstone and England amateur
international Jim Lewis ended with a
£3,000 sale to Norwich City. Returned to
his native Letchworth, Hertfordshire where
he continued to ply his trade as an
electrician, his trade before turning
professional.

## KJELDBERG, Jakob

*Appearances: 66 Goals: 2 (1993-1996)*
Career: *Chelsea (1993-1997).* Danish
international, was Glenn Hoddle's first
signing for the club when he paid
£400,000 to FC Silkborg. Good in the air
and quick, Kjeldberg took his time to
adjust to football in England's top flight but
once he settled, an effective partnership
with Erland Johnson was formed. Played in
the FA Cup Final defeat to Manchester
United and just as it seemed that he was
set for a long run in the team, a succession
of niggling injuries stopped him in his
tracks. His career never fully recovered. Is
now a popular television host in his home
land presenting football and reality TV
programmes and spends much of his time
living in the South of France. Presents the
popular Danish football magazine Onside.

## KNIGHT, Leon

*Appearances: 1 Goals: 0 (1999-2003)*
Career: *Chelsea, QPR, Huddersfield
Town, Sheffield Wed, Brighton, Swansea
City, Barnsley, MK Dons, Rushden &
Diamonds. (1999-2008).* Signed for the
Blues after trails as a youngster. The
cousin of Bolton defender Zat Knight,
spent five seasons at Stamford Bridge but
made his only first team appearance in the
UEFA Cup against Levski Sofia. Had spells
on loan, one of which, at Brighton, turned
into a permanent deal. The Blues received
£50,000 when the Seagulls were promoted
thanks to a Knight penalty in the play-off
final. Has never really settled in one place
and was released by Queen of the South
at the end of the 2009/10 season.

## KNOX, Tommy

*Appearances: 21 Goals: 0 (1962-1965)*
Career: *Chelsea, Newcastle United, Mansfield Town, Northampton Town. (1962-1969).* Was an East Stirling team mate of Eddie McCreadie and followed him to Stamford Bridge four months after his transfer. He struggled to get a regular first team game and had to wait two seasons for his chance to impress. A tricky winger, who was impressive in training but failed to reproduce his best form in first team matches. When Tommy Docherty decided to play three strikers he was left out in the cold completely and was sold to Newcastle United for £10,000. Is now living in the Basingstoke area.

Photo: Rod George

## LAKE, George

*Appearances: 1 Goals: 0 (1914-1918)*
Career: *Manchester City, Chelsea. (1913-1918).* A well built wing half who made his only first team outing against WBA in April 1914 and returned to the reserves for the last season before the outbreak of World War One. Was still registered as a Chelsea player when he became one of the last British 'Tommy's' to be killed in France before the armistice was signed in October 1918.

## LAMBOURDE, Bernard

*Appearances: 60 Goals: 3 (1997-2001)*
Career: *Chelsea, Portsmouth. (1997-2001).* Signed for £1.6 million from Bordeaux, he was able to play in a number of defensive and midfield positions. A valuable asset, but was sent off in only his second appearance. Went onto win League Cup and Charity Shield winner's medals before Claudio Ranieri deemed him to be surplus to requirements. Played his first and last games for the club against Manchester United. After retiring in 2003, he became a member of the French Beach Football squad. Now lives in the South of France and has invested in a company that sells hardware for motor homes.

## LANGLEY, Tommy

*Appearances: 152 Goals: 43 (1974-1980)*
Career: *Chelsea, Queens Park Rangers, Crystal Palace, Coventry City, Wolverhampton Wanderers, Aldershot, Exeter City. (1974-1989).* Broke into the first team aged just 16 years and nine months when he made his league debut. This was against Leicester City in the 1974-1975 season, which was to end in relegation, but it was another three years before he was fully established in the first team even though he had scored the goal at Wolves which clinched promotion back to the First Division. As partner to Steve Finnieston, he was the leading scorer in the first season back in the top flight, then scored 16 goals more in 1978-79 when the Blues were relegated. A rare bright spark, he was voted player of the year. Reluctantly sold to QPR for £425,000 in August 1980 by Geoff Hurst after failure to win promotion. After hanging up his boots, he worked for Nashua in Bracknell where he was in dealer sales for copiers and fax machines. Worked for Chelsea radio and then Channel Five Breakfast News as a football reporter. Now lives in Bagshot, Surrey, is a presenter on Chelsea TV's Matchnight Live and is a players agent.

**GUESS WHO?** - see page 150 for answers. *Photo: Rod George*

## LAUDROP, Brian

*Appearances: 11  Goals: 1 (1998)*
Career: *Chelsea. (1998-1999).* Named by Pele as one of the Greatest 125 Living Footballers, but Chelsea fans never saw the best of him during his brief injury ravaged stay at Stamford Bridge. He scored his only goal in the Cup Winners' Cup against Copenhagen, where he also had a brief stay after leaving SW6. Has business interests in Denmark including soccer schools with former Danish keeper Lars Hogh. also works as a Champions League commentator for TV3+.

## LAVERICK, Bobby

*Appearances: 7  Goals: 0 (1955-1959)*
Career: *Chelsea, Everton, Brighton, Coventry City. (1955-1963).* Spent two years as an amateur before turning professional although two years of his time at the club were lost to National Service with R.A.M.C. He made his league debut against WBA at outside left but with competition from Frank Blunstone, Mike Block and Jim Lewis, he was allowed to leave for Everton. Settled in Ashford, Kent. Is now retired after working as a salesman for the Smiths Crisps for 18 years and thena local builders merchants.

## LAW, Tommy

*Appearances: 319  Goals: 19 (1925-1939)*
Career: *Chelsea. (1925-1939).* Picked up for a bargain £10 from Scottish junior football after only playing five games. He spent a total of 14 seasons at Stamford Bridge and was a rock at the heart of the defence for ten of those seasons. Was one of eight Scots in the team when he made his debut against Portsmouth in September 1926. He rejected lucrative offers from France to stay with the club, where he earned far less. Upon retirement in 1939, Law worked in a shipyard but remained a keen Chelsea fan until his death in February 1976 aged 67.

*Photo: Stuart Fuller*

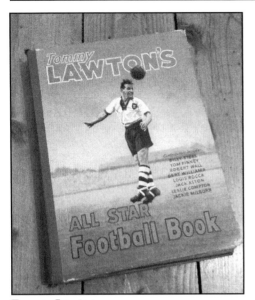

**Tommy Lawton**

# LAWTON, Tommy

*Appearances: 53  Goals: 35 (1945-1947)
Career: Burnley, Everton, Chelsea, Notts
County, Brentford, Arsenal. (1935-1955).*
One of the greatest English centre
forwards of all-time, Lawton was widely
seen at the complete player. A master in
the air and stunning on the floor, his
arrival at the club was supposed to signal
the start of a major challenge for honours.
One of a spate of big name signings, he
arrived from Everton in an £11,500 deal
and made his debut in a friendly against
Dynamo Moscow in front of 82,905 at
Stamford Bridge, scoring with a trademark
header. He went onto score 20 goals in 26
games, but couldn't settle in London. This
brought him into conflict with manager
Billy Birrell and to become the first
£20,000 transfer when he shocked the
football world by joining third division
Notts County when he was at the peak of
his powers. Was known as a 'goal scoring
machine', he later managed Notts County
and Brentford. Returned to Meadow Lane
as coach and then chief scout before
becoming a publican in Lowdham. Also
wrote a column for the Nottingham
Evening Post. Died in the town in
November 1996 aged 76.

# Le SAUX, Graeme

*Appearances: 312  Goals: 16 (1987-1993
and 1997-2003). Career: Chelsea,
Blackburn Rovers, Chelsea, Southampton.
(1987-2005).* Was spotted playing in his
native Jersey in 1987 by John Hollins  but
he had to wait two years for his debut.
This was on the left side of midfield
against Portsmouth. A tireless worker, his
first spell at the club came to an end in
controversy, when upset at being
continually subbed by Ian Porterfield, he
threw his shirt onto the ground, and was
soon sold to Blackburn soon afterwards
for £700,000. Returned six years later as
Britain's most expensive defender in a £5
million deal. His second spell was hit by
injuries, which caused him to miss the
Cup Winners' Cup and FA Cup finals but
he did get a winner's medal in 1988. Was
swapped with Southampton's Wayne
Bridge and £500,000 in 2003. Worked for
the BBC and still occasionally appears and
presents on BBC2's Working Lunch. In
2006, he joined ABN Bank's UK private
banking team in the role of Ambassador
for their Sports Desk. Has also appeared
on game and reality television shows.

**Graham Le Saux**

## LEADBETTER, James

*Appearances: 3 Goals: 0 (1949-1952)*
Career: *Chelsea, Brighton, Ipswich Town. (1949-1966).* A ball playing Scottish inside forward who spent three years at Stamford Bridge without becoming a first team regular. His true potential was never unearthed, but went on to enjoy much success with Ipswich Town. Worked as a newsagent, then as a salesman with Cadburys in Suffolk. Returned to Scotland in 1971 to work in his father's garage business then became a delivery driver for the Scotsman publications - retiring in 1993. He died in July 2006 aged 78.

Photo: Hannah Lee

## LEBOEUF, Frank

*Appearances: 204 Goals: 24 (1996-2001)*
Career: *Chelsea (1996-2001).* Glenn Hoddle paid £2.5 million to Racing Club Strasbourg to secure the signing because he wanted to play a 3-5-2 formation. The Frenchman took time to get used to the barrage of high balls into the box, but once the majestic defender settled, he quickly became a cult hero with the Stamford Bridge crowd. He proved to be deadly from the penalty spot, only missing three times in over 20 attempts. Formed a decent partnership with Michael Duberry when the club reverted to a flat back four. By the time he had left, his trophy haul stood at two FA Cups, Cup Winners Cup, League Cup, Super Cup and a Charity Shield. The former French international is now living in Los Angeles, USA, still plays for Hollywood United, the celebrity football team and is trying to make it as an actor, on the big screen and the stage.

## LEE, Colin

*Appearances: 223 Goals: 41 (1980-1987)*
Career: *Bristol City, Hereford United, Torquay United, Tottenham Hotspur, Chelsea, Brentford. (1974-1988).* When Sir Geoff Hurst needed a replacement for Bill Garner, he opened the cheque book and paid £200,000 to Spurs. Lee made his debut against Cardiff City and over the next five years was a regular in the starting line up. He helped the club to the second division title in 1984 before scoring two goals in the Full Members Cup Final against Manchester City. despite playing most of the season at full back because of the Kerry Dixon and David Speedie partnership. He suffered his fair share of hamstring injuries and was allowed to join Brentford to pursue his interest in coaching. Has managed Watford, Wolves, Torquay, Walsall and Millwall. Made a fortune as a property developer and was CEO at Torquay United until being placed in gardening leave at the end of the 2009-10 season.

*Photo: Rowan Farnham-Long*

## LEE, David

*Appearances: 194  Goals: 13 (1988-1998)*
Career: *Chelsea, Reading, Plymouth Argyle, Portsmouth, Sheffield United, Bristol Rovers, Crystal Palace, Exeter City. (1988-2000).* Spent a decade at Stamford Bridge and it is often thought that his versatility cost him a regular place in the team. He could play in central defence, full back, midfield or even up front and made a goal scoring debut against Leicester City. Was part of the Division Two title winning squad, largely in a supporting role though. In the First Division, he played alongside Graham Roberts and Ken Monkou and won rave reviews. Won a Full Members Cup winner's medal but his career stagnated until Paul Elliott was injured. Featured in the League Cup Final win over in 1998 but was allowed to leave on a free transfer to move back to his native Bristol, joining Rovers. David is now a full time development coach with Bristol City FC overseeing the 18-21 year-olds.

## LEE, John

*Appearances: 7  Goals: 1 (1920-1924)*
Career: *Hull City, Chelsea, Watford, Rotherham United. (1913-1927).* Signed for a high fee at the time (£1,500) and immediately broke into the first team squad but it was soon apparent that he wasn't really up to the demands of playing in the First Division. Returned to Hull where he lived and worked until his death in 1955.

*Photo: Nick Sarebi*

## LEWINGTON, Ray

*Appearances: 92  Goals: 4 (1974-1979)*
Career: *Chelsea, Wimbledon, Fulham, Sheffield United, Fulham. (1975-1989).* A ball winning midfielder who allowed the more skillful Ray Wilkins and Gary Stanley to flourish. Was an ever present in the 1976-77 Division Two promotion winning side, but he lacked the pace and skill to become a top class top flight player. When Danny Blanchflower replaced Ken Shellito, his days at the club were numbered and he was allowed to leave in 1979 to try his luck in Canada. Has since enjoyed a long career in coaching and management. He has managed Fulham, Brentford, Watford and has been back at Fulham since 2007.

Photo: Wally G

**GUESS WHO? - see page 150 for answers.** *Photo: Rod George*

## LEWIS, Fred

*Appearances: 26  Goals: 0 (1946-1953)*
Career: *Chelsea, Colchester United. (1946-1955).* A neat player who spent seven years at the club but mainly in the reserves. Having signed after serving in the Royal Navy during World War 2, he made his debut against Bolton Wanderers in August 1946 in place of Danny Winter. Left for Colchester United having failed to command a regular place. He later moved back to the Aylesbury area, where he died in 1975 after scouting for the club.

## LEWIS, Jim

*Appearances: 95  Goals: 40 (1952-1958)*
Career: *Leyton Orient, Chelsea. (1950-1958).* An amateur throughout his career, he joined Chelsea from leading non league club of the time, Walthamstow Avenue. While his team mates earned £12 a week, he received nothing. One of the best goal scoring wingers of his day, he shared the outside left birth with Frank Blunstone. Played 17 games and scored six goals in the 1955 Championship winning side, who all received a suit. He was presented with a plaque six years later, which has hung in his loo for over 50 years.. He also represented Great Britain at three Olympics Games. Worked as a travelling salesman selling Thermos Flasks, he later ran a pub in Southend and now lives in retirement in Essex.

## LIVESY, Charlie

*Appearances: 42  Goals: 18 (1959-1961)*
Career: *Southampton, Chelsea, Gillingham, Watford, Northampton Town, Brighton. (1956-1969).* Joined The Blues in May 1959 from Southampton for £20,000 plus Cliff Huxford. Scored eight goals in his first 14 games but despite his decent scoring record, he was replaced by Ron Tindall and sold to Gillingham for just £2,000 in 1961. Returned to his native east London where he became a painter and decorator. Died in St Bart's Hospital after a short illness in February 2005.

## LIVINGSTONE, Steve

*Appearances: 1  Goals: 0 (1993-1994)*
Career: *Coventry City, Blackburn Rovers, Chelsea, Port Vale, Grimsby Town, Carlisle United. (1986-2004).* Signed for £350,000 as part of the deal which took Graeme Le Saux to Blackburn Rovers. His stay in SW6 lasted just six months and his only first team appearance was as a sub against Manchester United at Old Trafford. He was off-loaded to Gillingham in October 1993 for just £130,000. Has since returned to his home-town, Middlesbrough, where he has invested in property. He still keeps in contact with his former club Grimsby Town, and took his 16 year old son down for a trial.

## LIVINGSTONE, William

*Appearances: 22  Goals: 0 (1955-1959)*
Career: *Reading, Chelsea, Brentford. (1949-1960).* One to never back out of a challenge, he always gave 100 per cent as a more than able deputy for Stan Wicks. Moved on as soon as John Mortimore emerged from the amateur ranks. The Scotsman lived in the same road as John Sillett in Wandsworth before moving back to the Reading area where he worked as an electrician until he retired, now lives in Tilehurst.

## LLOYD, Barry

*Appearances: 10  Goals: 0 (1966-1969)*
Career: *Chelsea, Fulham, Hereford United, Brentford. (1966-1978).* Joined his local club and made his debut against WBA in April 1967. With too many players battling for the same position he found his first team chances restricted and was sold to Fulham for £30,000 plus John Dempsey in 1968. Managed Yeovil and Worthing before joining Brighton as assistant manager in July 1986. The following January he was appointed manager, staying until May 1993. Worked at a BMW dealership in Worthing. Rejoined Brighton in 2007 and is now their youth team scout.

## LOCKE, Gary

*Appearances: 317 Goals: 4 (1972-1989)*
Career: *Chelsea, Crystal Palace. (1971-1986).* Won the Blues Player of the Year award in 1974 and shone like in a beacon, even though the club were relegated a the following season. Was an ever present when they won promotion two years later, after becoming a pillar of strength in the middle of the back four. Suffered from injuries towards the end of his stay at the club and was eventually replaced by Joey Jones. Moved to New Zealand where he still lives and works as an advertising executive for a newspaper.

## LUKE, George

*Appearances: 1 Goals: 0 (1967-1968)*
Career: *Newcastle United, Chelsea (1967-1968).* Arrived at Stamford Bridge three weeks after signing a professional contract at Newcastle's St James Park, in a part exchange deal involving Tommy Robson. Played his only league game against Leicester City in May 1967 but with Ron Harris, John Hollins and John Boyle already at the club, he could not make the breakthrough and quit the game aged 20. He emigrated to South Africa before returning home in 1976. After a spell playing under Barry Bridges in Ireland, he went to work for Wimpey Homes as chief buyer before setting up his own business in the building industry.

## LYON, Frank

*Appearances: 6 Goals: 0 (1907-1908)*
Career: *Stockport County, Crewe Alexandra, Watford, QPR, Chelsea, Crewe Alexandra. (1897-1909).* A full back who was known for his natural pace, started the 1907-1908 season as first choice until being ousted by new signing Frank Cameron. Returned to his home town club, Crewe, where a knee injury forced him into an early retirement. Opened his own business in the town, where he continued to live until his death in 1955.

## MACAULEY, James

*Appearances: 94 Goals: 5 (1940-1951)*
Career: *Chelsea, Aldershot Town. (1940-1952).* A hard working full back who made his debut for the club during the War when he served in the RAF,. He then enjoyed three seasons in the first team during peacetime, as a part timer, until he was replaced by Frank Mitchell. Had worked as a customs officer before joining the Blues and continued to work as a civil servant in London after the war.

## MACFARLANE, Ian

*Appearances: 43 Goals: 0 (1956-1958)*
Career: *Aberdeen, Chelsea, Leicester City, (1956-1958).* Was plucked from Aberdeen reserves and was a regular in the first team in his first season in English football. It was only a loss of form in his second season that resulted in his £9,000 sale to Leicester City. Later returned to Filbert Street to become assistant manager to both Frank McLintock and Jock Wallace. Also held the number two position at Middlesbrough, Man City and Sunderland before holding full charge at Carlisle. Later became chief scout at Leeds United. The scotsman is now back home and is now honorary president of Dunbarton FC.

## MACHIN, Alex

*Appearances: 61 Goals: 9 (1944-1948)*
Career: *Chelsea, Plymouth Argyle. (1945-1952).* Spotted playing in an Army match while serving in the Royal Hampshire Regiment during the Second World War. Was signed up on a full time contract when he was demobbed from the Army. A ferocious tackler, he spent one and a half seasons in the half back line before Ken Armstrong moved back and took his place. He left to start a new life in the West Country, where he had played his final league football with Plymouth Argyle. He worked as a postman in Cornwall until his retirement. He sadly died in 2005 aged 85.

**GUESS WHO?** - see page 150 for answers. *Photo: Rod George*

## MALCOLM, Andy

*Appearances: 28 Goals: 1 (1961-1962)*
Career: *West Ham United, Chelsea, Queens Park Rangers (1950-1964).* Was signed by Tommy Docherty early in his reign when it became obvious that he had a battle against relegation on his hands, so Ron Tindall plus £10,000 was sent to Upton Park. Immediately he was appointed skipper in the absence of Peter Sillett, but all too soon, it became obvious that relegation was inevitable. There was to be no place for him in the long term at Stamford Bridge and following a contract dispute with Docherty, he was sold to QPR in October 1962. Ran three pubs in Essex but has been living in Port Elizabeth in South Africa since 1986.

## MARSH, Wilson

*Appearances: 12 Goals: 0 (1921-1924)*
Career: *Chelsea (1921-1924).* Had the misfortune to be back-up to three quality goalkeepers Jim Molyneux, Colin Hampton and the great Corinthian Howard Baker during his time at the club. Made 11 of his 12 appearances in the 1923-24 season but was allowed to leave to join Dundee in 1924. Became a champion golfer on the Scottish circuit and was 95 when he died in 1989.

## MATTHEW, Damian

*Appearances: 27 Goals: 0 (1989-1994)*
Career: *Chelsea, Luton T, Crystal Palace, Bristol Rovers, Burnley, Northampton T. (1989-1998).* A creative midfielder who spent six years at Stamford Bridge. Only played 27 games, despite forming a decent partnership with Graham Stuart. Even the appointment of a cultured player like Glenn Hoddle couldn't kick start his career and he was forced to seek a fresh start at Crystal Palace. After a back injury ended his career, he returned to the Bridge and spent six years as youth development officer before taking on a similar role at Charlton Athletic, where he is now also looking after the reserves.

## MATTHEWS, Reg

*Appearances: 148 Goals: 0 (1956-1961)*
Career: *Coventry City, Chelsea, Derby County(1950-1967).* Had won five England caps as a Third Division player by the time that Ted Brake bought him to Stamford Bridge for £20,000 in 1956, a then record fee for a goalkeeper. He produced a string of top displays but in the end lost his place to Peter Bonetti and was sold to Derby County. Later worked for Massey Ferguson Ltd for twenty years before having to retire through ill health died in Coventry in October 2001 aged 67.

Photo: Crystian Cruz

## MAYBANK, Teddy

*Appearances: 32 Goals: 6 (1974-1976)*
*Career: Chelsea, Fulham, Brighton, Fulham. (1974-1979).* A tall blond striker who made his league debut in a relegation battle with Spurs at White Hart Lane in April 1975. However, when the club dropped into the second division, he struggled to adapt and manager at the time, Eddie McCreadie, turned to Steve Finnieston. This added to the fact that a young Tommy Langley was waiting in the wings, he was allowed to join Fulham for £75,000, despite still only being 20 years old. Later played for Brighton and back at Craven Cottage before hanging up his boots. Started the Maybank Press, publishing company and printed football programmes after is career was ended early through injury. Since then he has worked in construction and has appeared on TV shows Blind Date and The Weakest Link. Is now believed to have varied business interests on the South Coast.

## MAYES, Alan

*Appearances: 76 Goals: 24 (1980-1983)*
*Career: Queens Park, Rangers, Watford, Northampton Town, Swindon Town, Chelsea, Swindon Town, Carlisle United, Newport County, Blackpool. (1971-1987)..* Arrived at Stamford Bridge for £200,000 in December 1980 with a reputation in the lower divisions for being a free scorer. This is exactly what was needed to breath some much needed life into a faltering promotion campaign, but he couldn't flourish in a side that was low on confidence and being the small side he was never going to produce his best form on a constant supply of high balls. In the end, was allowed to leave on a free transfer as John Neal looked to offload players to rebuild the side. Worked in the commercial department at Wycombe Wanderers, then became sales manager for the Cavendish Group. Is still working in the hospitality business, but now for Ambro Events.

## McALISTER, Kevin

*Appearances: 140 Goals: 13 (1985-1991)*
*Career: Chelsea. (1985-1991).* Became John Neal's last ever signing for the club when the manager paid Falkirk £35,000 to bring him south of the border just before handing over control of first team affairs to John Hollins. Despite being an old fashioned winger with good ball control and a wide range of skills, he was forced to live in the shadow of Pat Nevin for three seasons because of his fellow Scots better goal scoring record. Once Nevin had been sold to Everton, McALISTER seized the chance to become first choice. Enjoyed success during his stay in SW6 winning a Full Members Cup, a Second Division Champion winner's medal and Zenith Data Systems Cup, before returning to Scotland where he played for another fourteen years. Was player manager of Albion Rovers before becoming Chelsea's Scotland scout. He is now Brechin City's assistant manager.

## McANDREW, Tony

*Appearances: 23 Goals: 4 (1982-1984)*
*Career: Middlesbrough, Chelsea, Middlesbrough, Darlington, Hartlepool United, (1973-1988).* John Neal's captain at Middlesbrough arrived at Stamford Bridge for a tribunal set fee of £92,500 in a bid to add some security at the back. A rock solid defender and naturally aggressive player, he took the captain's arm-band for a spell as the team marched to the Second Division Championship. His career at the club was wrecked by a string of injuries and when he finally regained fitness he was unable to win back his place in the starting line up. This led to being shipped back to Boro in 1984 in a swap deal involving Darren Wood. Worked as a rep for a North East brewery has coached the youth teams at Darlington, Leicester City and Stoke City. Has been enjoying his second stint at Aston Villa since 1999.

## McAULEY Bob

*Appearances: 74  Goals: 1 (1932-1936)*
Career: *Chelsea, Cardiff City, Workington (1932-1939).* Arrived in London with a massive reputation but he rarely lived up to his billing. Spent the first two seasons in the shadow of Tommy Law, Les Odell and George Barber, but then played 40 games in 1934-35 season before moving to Wales. After World War 2 he became a scout for Rangers in North East Scotland until his retirement in 1979. Continued to live in Glasgow until his death in 1994.

## McCALLIOG, Jim

*Appearances: 12  Goals: 3 (1963-1965)*
Career: *Chelsea, Sheffield Wednesday, Wolverhampton Wanderers, Manchester United, Southampton, Lincoln City. (1964-1978).* Signed at Chelsea after a short spell at Leeds United where he was an amateur. Never quite fitted the bill at Stamford Bridge, only making a handful of first team appearances. Made his debut on his 18th birthday in a League Cup clash with Birmingham City but was sold in October 1965 to Sheffield Wednesday a £37,500. This was a record fee at the time for a teenager. Had spells as manager of Halifax Town and Runcorn but then became journalist and publican in Wetherby and York. He now has a pub in Fenwick, Ayrshire

## McCONNELL, English

*Appearances: 22  Goals: 0 (1910-1911)*
Career: *Sunderland, Sheffield Wed, Chelsea. (1905-1912).* Purchased from Sheffield Wednesday in 1910. £500 was paid immediately with the rest as an IOU. He was one of several signings that the club made in a bid to beat the drop and as a result, the transfer deadline was introduced. He played 22 consecutive games for the club but a cartilage operation spelled the end of his stay. Moved to Belfast after his career ended and went into business until his death in June 1928 aged 45.

## McCREADIE, Eddie

*Appearances: 410  Goals: 5 (1962-1974)*
Career: *Chelsea (1959-1975).* Arrived from East Stirling as an unknown in April 1962. Within 12 months, his partnership with Ken Shellito was key to the club returning to the top flight.  Tommy Docherty described him as "the best left back in Europe" and within two years, standing in as a centre forward for the injured Barry Bridges, he scored the winning goal of the first leg of the League Cup Final after a stunning 80 yard run. Endured a stormy relationship with Docherty and had five transfer requests rejected. Suffered FA Cup heart break in 1967 but played a vital role in the success over Leeds three years later. Succeeded Ron Harris as skipper and joined the coaching staff in the summer of 1974. Went onto manage Chelsea before moving to the USA to take charge of Memphis Rogues. Then became a painter and decorator but has now retired and lives on a ranch in Tennessee.

## McFARLANE, Alex

*Appearances: 4  Goals: 0 (1913-1915)*
Career: *Arsenal, Newcastle United, Chelsea (1896-1915).* Was just establishing himself at Stamford Bridge when the Great War broke out and only made one appearance after hostilities. Became a successful manager in between the wars with two spells at both Dundee and Charlton Athletic. Drifted out of football at the age of 57 after a stint at Blackpool, moved back to Scotland in retirement, where he died.

## McINNES, John

*Appearances: 37  Goals: 5 (1947-1951)*
Career: *Chelsea. (1947-1951).* Faced an almost constant battle against injury and illness in his five years at the club. A fast and direct player, but he didn't become the player that his talent deserved. He ended his career at non-league Bedford Died in the town in 1973 aged just 46.

Photo: Dennis Wareing

## McKENZIE, Duncan

*Appearances: 16 Goals: 4 (1978-1979)*
Career: *Nottingham Forest, Mansfield Town, Leeds United, Everton, Chelsea, Blackburn Rovers. (1968-1981).* One of the classiest players to have graced the League during the seventies. McKenzie became the club's first major signing for four years when severe financial problems had restricted transfer expenditure. He was brought in in the hope of finding a much needed cutting edge, but he never looked at home playing in a side with limited ability. Accordingly, he struggled to produce his best form and after only seven months in the capital was sold to Blackburn Rovers for less than half of the £165,000 originally paid out to Everton. Now working for Football in the Community based at Everton. Lives in Newton-le-Willow, Merseyside, owned a delicatessen, and has become an accomplished after dinner speaker and newspaper columnist.

## McKNIGHT, Phillip

*Appearances: 33 Goals: 1 (1947-1954)*
Career: *Chelsea, Leyton Orient (1947-1961).* 'Corky' moved south and joined Chelsea after leaving the Navy. A long throw expert, he spent eight seasons at the club, making his league debut against Portsmouth in May 1948 as a hard working, ever reliable wing half. Coached the Orient 'A' team before going into management with Hayes and then Ruislip Manor. He went on to become a businessman in the London area.

## McLAUGHLIN, Joe

*Appearances: 268 Goals: 7 (1983-1989)*
Career: *Chelsea, Charlton Athletic, Watford. (1972-1983).* John Neal paid £100,000 to Morton to bring the athletic Scot to London. He immediately formed a defensive partnership with Colin Pates, helping the club to a Second Division Championship. Over the next five seasons in SW6 he was an automatic selection as a lynchpin at the back. He won a Full Members Cup medal in 1986 and another Division Two Championship in 1989 just months before Charlton paid a club record £650,000 to take him across the capital after Ken Monkou was brought in to partner David Lee. Went into coaching, with Millwall, and Morton but is now based in Glasgow running his own business recruiting young players for US universities. Also scouts for Bolton.

## McMILLAN, Eric

*Appearances: 5 Goals: 0 (1958-1960)*
Career: *Chelsea, Hull City, Halifax Town, Scarborough. (1958-1969).* A mobile wing half who was signed on amateur forms after he served in the RAF. Was never comfortable in the First Division and only made a handful of appearances as a result after making his debut against Burnley in September 1959. He was sold to Hull in the following closed season for £2,000. Returned to live and work in Hull as a postman. He retired and sadly died in March 2006 aged 69.

## McMILLAN, Paul

*Appearances: 1  Goals: 0 (1967-1968)*
Career: *Chelsea. (1967-1968).* A Glasgow
born wing half who turned professional in
July 1967 and made his league debut
against Southampton in a 6-2 defeat. That
was in the September, but by February
1968 he had been advised to quit the
game by doctors because of illness. He
returned to Scotland where he worked on
the coaching staff at Clydebank.

## McNALLY, Errol

*Appearances: 9  Goals: 0 (1961-1963)*
Career: *Chelsea. (1961-1963).* Was one of
a string of goalkeepers signed to provide
support for Peter Bonetti when Tommy
Docherty paid Portadown £5,000 to
secure his signature in December 1961.
Made his league debut in the 4-0
drubbing suffered at the hands of Everton
in March 1962 as the club hurtled towards
relegation. Was released after a handful
appearances and returned to Northern
Ireland to join Glenavon. Became Export
Sales Manager for Barbour Threads in
Lisburn until his retirement in 2002. He
continues to live in County Down.

## McNAUGHT, John

*Appearances: 13  Goals: 2 (1986-1987)*
Career: *Chelsea. (1986-1987).* Signed for
£80,000 from Hamilton in April 1986 and
made his debut in the 5-1 defeat at the
hands of Watford in a team that contained
eight Scotsman. His time at the club was
blighted by disciplinary problems - in 34
first team and reserve games he was sent
off twice and booked eleven times. He
also started a tunnel brawl after a reserve
game with Arsenal, walked out on the club
in the autumn of 1987 and returned to
Scotland. Voted Hamilton's all time cult
hero, he had a spell working as a
nightclub doorman after his career was
ended with a serious blood disorder that
needed a kidney transplant. Despite
appearing to be back in full health, he died
suddenly in June 1997 at the age of 32.

## McNICHOL, John

*Appearances: 202  Goals: 66 (1952-1958)*
Career: *Newcastle United, Brighton,
Chelsea, Crystal Palace. (1946-1962).*
More than a few eyebrows were raised
when McNichol became Ted Drake's first
signing for the club. He joined for £15,000
from Brighton in August 1952 and was a
27 year-old who had played all of his
football in the Third Division. Against the
odds, it proved to be a very shrewd
investment as he made the step up in
class with a minimum amount of fuss, only
missing six games in his first three
seasons at the club. His partnership with
Roy Bentley was integral in the 1955
Championship winning success, before
moving onto Crystal Palace. Owned a
newsagent's shop and worked in the fund-
raising departments of Crystal Palace and
Brighton & Hove Albion before retiring to
Saltdean near Brighton.

## MEEHAN, Tommy

*Appearances: 133  Goals: 4 (1920-1924)*
Career: *Rochdale, Manchester United,
Chelsea. (1917-1924).* Arrived from
Manchester United for £3,300 after
lengthy negotiations and became a crowd
idol almost as soon as he made his debut
against Liverpool just after Christmas in
1920. A 'jack in a box' type of player, he
was always likely to pop up anywhere and
was seen as a live-wire. He was a regular
in the half back line for four seasons and
had won his first international cap for
England against Ireland just before his
death when he was at the height of his
powers. Despite this, he was unable to
help stop the club dropping into the
Second Division. Died in St Georges
Hospital in August 1924 from polio. His
death shocked the football world and
2,000 mourners attended his funeral in
Wandsworth. A fund was set up to support
his wife and children and a benefit match
between Chelsea and a London XI raised
more than £1,500 with more money
donated later.

# MEDHURST Harry

*Appearances: 157 Goals: 0 (1946-1952)*
Career: *West Ham United, Chelsea, Brighton. (1938-1952).* When Chelsea needed to replace the legendary Vic Woodley, they looked no further than across the capital to West Ham. Medhurst had lost his place to Ernie Gregory, so a swap deal involving Joe Payne was set up. Despite being over 30, he immediately established himself as the number one keeper at the club and gave superb service over the next five years. A fruit farmer and landscape gardener by profession he served as assistant trainer, physio and trainer until his retirement in 1975, nine years before his death in Woking, Surrey in April 1984 aged 68.

# MELCHIOT, Mario

*Appearances: 165 Goals: 5 (1999-2004)*
Career: *Chelsea, Birmingham City, Wigan Athletic. (1999-2010).* The Dutch international arrived at Stamford Bridge on a Bosman free transfer after coming through the ranks at Ajax. An attacking minded right wing back, he was an FA Cup winner in his first season at the club despite only making a handful of first team appearances in the Premier League. He held down a regular first team place from 2000 until his departure on a free transfer under Jose Mourinho. Joined Umm-Salal

Sports Club of the Qatari Stars League who are managed by former Chelsea coach Henk ten Cate in June 2010 after his Latics deal ended. Before joining the Blues he released a rap/R&B track called Midas Touch with his then team mates Benni McCarthy and Dean Gore calling themselves BMD.

# MIDDLEBOE, Nils

*Appearances: 46 Goals: 0 (1913-1921)*
Career: *Newcastle United, Chelsea. (1913-1921).* Signed for Chelsea after permission from Newcastle when he was introduced to the club by another great amateur Vivian Woodward. The first non-British player in the clubs history made his debut against Derby County in November 1913 and was appointed captain despite never having played for the club before. A true amateur, he wasn't required by the club to travel to away games and even his appearances at home were too infrequent during his nine years at the club. Whenever he played for the Danish national team during his time in the capital he always gave the name of his team as KB never as Chelsea! He kept in touch with the club and was a guest at the 1967 FA Cup Final, some 54 years after leaving. A qualified lawyer, he worked as a banker during his stay in London and was the first ever scorer for the Danish national team. He died in Copenhagen in September 1976 aged 89.

# MILLAR, John

*Appearances: 11 Goals: 0 (1984-1987)*
Career: *Chelsea, Northampton Town, Blackburn Rovers (1984-1991).* A London University Student, he captained the youth team before graduating from the reserves into the first team squad. Made his debut at left back aged 19 in a home defeat to Oxford United in February 1986 but was later converted into a left sided midfielder. Was allowed to join Blackburn Rovers in 1987. Finished his career in his native Scotland and is now living in Coatbridge.

Photo: Feggy Art

## MILLS, George

*Appearances: 239 Goals: 123 (1929-1943) Career: Chelsea. (1929-1943).* A bargain £10 signing from non league Bromley, Mills became the first player in the clubs history to score 100 league goals. Often overlooked in favour of more glamourous players like Hughie Gallagher, Joe Payne and Joe Bambrick, he was never out gunned by them. Earned a nickname of 'The Bomb' and scored 14 goals in his first season to help the club win promotion to the First Division. A tall well built striker, he gave fantastic service and even managed to score a hat trick on his international debut for England. Continued to find his chances limited despite his scoring record for Chelsea. Returned to Stamford Bridge after the Second World War as a coach, later worked for a printing company in the City of London. Died suddenly on holiday in Torquay in July 1970 aged 61.

## MINTO, Scott

*Appearances: 72 Goals: 5 (1994-1997) Career: Charlton Athletic, Chelsea, West Bromwich Albion, Rotherham United. (1989-2006).* Glenn Hoddle paid Charlton Athletic £775,000 to help solve a perceived weakness at left back despite having Andy Myers and Frank Sinclair in the squad. His time at Stamford Bridge was hit by injury and illness and an Achilles tendon injury meant he had to wait four months to make his debut for the club. This proved to be a sign of things to come as he continued to battle away, until Graeme Le Saux's recruitment made the task even harder. He couldn't agree a new deal with the club and left for Benfica in 1997 after making one of his last appearances in the FA Cup Final victory over Middlesbrough at Wembley. Now works as an unpaid driver for a Rotherham hospice, and is also a pundit for Sky Television appearing on a variety of programmes.

## MITCHELL, David

*Appearances: 8 Goals: 0 (1989-1991) Career: Chelsea, Newcastle United, Swindon Town, Millwall. (1989-1995).* The Scotland born Australian international striker was a £200,000 signing from Dutch side Feyenoord to provide cover for Kerry Dixon and Gordon Durie. He had problems adjusting to the pace of English football despite being given a run in the team and never really settled. A string of injuries didn't help his cause nor did a spell on loan at Newcastle United and he was eventually sold to Swindon Town in 1991. After a spell with Millwall, Mitchell returned to Australia where he coached Sydney Olympic, Sydney United and Parramatta Power before being appointed assistant manager of Perth Glory. He stepped into the manager's hot seat in November 1997 and has been there ever since. In the past he has also scouted for Feyenoord, helped coach the Australian Olympic team and worked as a television pundit for Fox Sports.

## MITCHELL, Frank

*Appearances: 85 Goals: 1 (1949-1952) Career: Birmingham City, Chelsea, Watford. (1943-1958).* Strangely, this 'Mitchell' was born in Australia but moved to England as a teenager (see David, above). He developed into a classy wing half, but saw his career destroyed like so many good players by the Second World War. Spent three seasons in the Blues' first team after signing from Birmingham City, looked set for a long stay at the club until he lost his place to Bill Dickson and was sold for £7,000 to Watford. Played county cricket with Warwickshire, was groundsman and secretary for Knowle and Dorridge cricket club and by day his job was coaching and keeping the grounds at Kynoch's which he did for many years. Died in Myton Hamlet in April 1984 aged 61.

# M

## MOLYNEUX, Jim

*Appearances: 239  Goals: 0 (1910-1922)*
Career: *Stockport County, Chelsea, Stockport County. (1906-1925).* When Chelsea found themselves back in Division Two they needed a goalkeeper to provide back up to Jack Whitley. accordingly, they paid Stockport £550 for the 23 year-old stopper, who soon became established as first choice between the posts. He saw off competition from Whitley and Ron Brebner in his second season to win an FA Cup winner's up medal. He soon developed into one of the best keepers in the country and became a firm favourite with the fans. Went on to help the club win the London Victory Cup against Fulham in 1919. By the time he left the club he had kept  a total of 77 clean sheets in 239 first team appearances. Suffered shrapnel wounds whilst serving at Ypres in the First World War but within two months was back in action. Later worked for the Stockport Electricity Department for 20 years. Died in January 1950 aged 65.

## MONKOU, Ken

*Appearances: 119  Goals: 2 (1989-1992)*
Career: *Chelsea, Southampton, Huddersfield Town. (1989-2001).* A bargain basement signing after Chelsea beat off competition from two German and one Dutch club to sign the classy defender for £100,000. They have him time to settle in before blooding him at the start of the 1989/90 season in a five man defence. Playing in the centre with Graham Roberts and David Lee, he quickly became a pillar of strength and won a Zenith Data Systems Cup winners medal in 1990. He also became the first black player to be named the club's Player of the Season and it wasn't until the arrival of Paul Elliott that he was pushed out of the first team picture and not before an unsuccessful attempt to play him at left back. Now splits his time between Yorkshire and London and ran a pancake house in Oude Delft, back in his native Holland.

*Photo: Rowan Farnham-Long*

Monkou runs his own management company, is an active ambassador for anti-racism and can be seen on TV in Holland and Chelsea TV. While 'up north', it is reported that this former solid defender spends his time enjoying a far more peaceful hobby... fly fishing!

## MOORE, Graham

*Appearances: 72  Goals: 14 (1961-1963)*
Career: *Cardiff City, Chelsea, Manchester United, Northampton Town, Charlton Athletic, Doncaster Rovers. (1958-1973)..* Signed as a 20 year old by Tommy Docherty for a club record £35,000 in December 1961 from financially stricken Cardiff City as he looked to breath some life in into a campaign which ended in relegation with Moore netting only twice. The club bounced back at the first attempt but he still found the target hard to find, only chipping in with eight goals. With Barry Bridges and Bobby Tambling becoming the preferred partnership, patience was soon lost and he was sold to Manchester United for the same amount as the club had originally paid out. The Welsh international midfielder was a miner at Penallta Colliery before turning professional but went on to run a couple of pubs when he left the game. Later became a sub post office in Scarborough until retiring.

## MORAIS, Nuno

*Appearances: 16 Goals: 0 (2004-2007)*
Career: *Chelsea. (2004-2007).* A defensive midfielder who signed for an undisclosed fee from Portuguese outfit FC Penafiel. He found chances limited despite being an under-21 international and spent much of his time in the reserves. Made his first team debut against Scunthorpe United in the FA Cup but was released in May 2007. He has been playing for Cypriot champions Apoel since leaving Stamford Bridge.

## MORRIS, Jody

*Appearances: 173 Goals: 9 (1995-2003)*
Career: *Chelsea, Leeds United, Rotherham United, Millwall. (1995-2007).* A close friend of John Terry after the pair had come through the youth and reserve team ranks together, he was an FA Cup winner in 2000 after coming on as a late substitute. Was even made club skipper for a short while by Gianluca Vialli but never had a settled first team place, often overlooked in favour of bigger and more glamourous names. Was offered a five year deal by the club in 2003 but choose to turn it down, shook hands on a move to Blackburn before it fell through and he joined Leeds instead. He has been playing in Scotland for St Johnstone after unsuccessful trials with Charlton Athletic and Brentford. Was voted in the top 50 worst footballers to grace the Premier League.

*Photo: wkocian*

## MORTIMORE, John

*Appearances: 279 Goals: 10 (1956-1965)*
Career: *Chelsea, Queens Park Rangers, Sunderland. (1955-1967).* Signed as a replacement for Ken Armstrong at right half but became most effective in central defender. Strong in the air and useful on the ground, he became established in the side in 1957 but lost his place twice to Bobby Evans and then Mel Scott even though both players were widely seen as not being in the same class. Regained his spot, was an ever present in the 1963 Second Division promotion winning side and was a League Cup winner two years later. Sold to Southampton for £8,000 in the same year, in September 1965. Worked as a teacher for several years after leaving the club, managed Portsmouth, Benfica (twice), Real Betis, Belenenses, and was caretaker boss of Southampton. While in Portugal, he won the national championship in both 1976–77 and 1986–87, and the Portuguese Cup in 1986 and 1987. Also coached at Sunderland, Chelsea and Southampton, where he became club president. Is now retired and living in Romsey.

## MULHOLLAND, Jimmy

*Appearances: 12 Goals: 3 (1962-1964)*
Career: *Chelsea, Stockport County, Crewe Alexandra. (1962-1971).* Came down from Scotland to join the club from East Stirling for £8,000 in October 1962. Despite a promising start to his career in west London, he struggled against more experienced defenders and was allowed to return 'north of the border' to join Greenock Morton in a part exchange deal which saw Billy Sinclair travelling in the opposite direction. Is believed to have remained in Scotland at the end of his career but suffered from ill health before his reported death in June 1994 aged 56.

## MULLIGAN, Paddy

*Appearances: 79 Goals: 2 (1969-1972)*
*Career: Chelsea, Crystal Palace, West Bromwich Albion. (1969-1977).* Moved across the Irish Sea from Shamrock Rovers for a then record fee for a Republic of Ireland player of £17,500 in October 1969. It took the former office furniture salesman time to get his fitness levels up to First Division standards and take advantage of Eddie McCreadie's long term injury problems. An attacking right back who was an expert at over lapping, was a second half substitute in the Cup Winners Cup Final win over Real Madrid in Athens in 1971, then his absence from the second half of the League Cup Final against Stoke City in 1972 is widely seen to have contributed to the teams defeat. Rarely assured of his place in the team, but it was still disappointing when he jumped at the chance of regular first team football and joined Crystal Palace for £75,000 in 1972. Became an insurance agent in West London, then returned to Ireland to manage Galway and Shelbourne in the mid-80's. Opened his own accountancy-insurance business. Also a pundit for Dublin based Newstalk Sport.

## MURPHY, Jerry

*Appearances: 39 Goals: 3 (1985-1988)*
*Career: Crystal Palace, Chelsea. (1976-1987).* A member of Terry Venables exciting young Palace side dubbed the 'Team of the Eighties', he was John Hollins first signing for the club on a free transfer. Wretched luck with injuries kept him from being a first team regular for much of his time at Stamford Bridge. He impressed on his home debut against Coventry City, only to lose his place through injury. Competition from Kevin McALISTER and Mickey Hazard restricted his appearances in his first season, while fitness problems limited him to 13 games in his final two seasons before his contract was cancelled in the summer of 1988. A Republic of Ireland international, he emigrated to Australia but then returned to coach disadvantaged kids in his native East London.

**Paddy Mulligan (3rd from left, back row)** *Photo: Soccer C*

**GUESS WHO?** - see page 150 for answers. *Photo: Rod George*

## MURRAY, Bert

*Appearances: 183  Goals: 44 (1961-1966)*
*Career: Chelsea, Birmingham City,
Brighton, Peterborough United. (1961-
1975).* An outside right when he came into
the first team in October 1961 before
being converted into a right back by
Tommy Docherty and Dave Sexton.
Established himself in the team at the
expense of Peter Brabrook, to form a
formidable partnership with Ken Shellito.
He was even a dependable emergency
goalkeeper when needed. Played in
midfield when Docherty switched to a 4-
3-3 formation and his 17 goals in 1964-
1965 was the highest total from a winger
since Dick Spence chipped in with 19
goals 30 years previously. A League Cup
winner, he saw his saw his time at the club
ended by the emergence of Peter Osgood
and was sold to Birmingham City for
£25,000. The former England under-23
international went onto become a publican
at the White Horse and then the Bull in
Market Deeping, Lincolnshire.

*Photo: http://www.toscanafotonotizie.it*

## MUTU, Adrian

*Appearances: 38  Goals: 10 (2003-2004)*
*Career: Chelsea. (2003-2004).* Signed
from Parma for £15.8 million as part of a
massive spending spree at the start of

Roman Abrammovich's reign at the club,
he started his career at the club on fire,
with four goals in his first three games, but
they didn't quite flow quite as freely
afterwards. He fell out with Jose Mourinho
in his early days at the club when they
accused each other of lying over the
striker's fitness for a World Cup qualifier.
Then, in September 2004, he tested
positive for cocaine, was sacked the
following month and the FA handed him a
seven month ban and a £20,000 fine.
Returned to play in Italy after his ban ended,
joining Juventus and then Fiorentina,
where he has been since 2006. Was given
a further nine month ban after failing a
second drugs test, and has been fighting
Chelsea being awarded €17.178m as a
breach of contract. The club are also
entitled to charge 5% interest and he
faces another ban if the money isn't paid.

## MYERS, Andy

*Appearances: 106  Goals: 2 (1991-1999)*
*Career: Chelsea, Bradford City,
Portsmouth, Colchester United, Brentford.
(1991-2005).* Joined the club as a 13 year-
old after trails with Arsenal and Watford.
Four years later, he became the youngest
debutant since Tommy Langley. He started
his first team career in midfield but his
real break came when he was switched to
left back in the place of Tommy Boyd. This
enabled him to establish himself in the
first team. A serious ankle injury cost him
the best part of two seasons and when he
regained his fitness he played on the left
side of central defence alongside Michael
Duberry and David Lee. He was sold to
Bradford in July 1999 to search out regular
football after Scott Minto took his left wing
back role. Has business interests that
included a company which supplies air
conditioning, electrical blinds and
curtains, and another which supplies high
end entertainment equipment in houses.
Clients are said to include John Terry. His
business partners are Jody Morris and
Michael Duberry.

*Photo: In The City*

## NEVIN, Pat

*Appearances: 242 Appearances: 45 (1983-1988). Career: Chelsea, Everton, Tranmere Rovers. (1983-1997).*

One of the most stylish and creative players of his day. Rejected by Celtic as a youngster for being too small, he arrived at Stamford Bridge for £95,000 from Clyde in July 1983 as part of John Neal's rebuilding plans and was an immediate success. He scored 14 goals in his first season, picking up a Second Division Championship winner's medal, as well as being named the club's Player of the Year. In the First Division, he was the main provider of ammunition for Kerry Dixon and David Speedie. Won a Full Members Cup winners medal in 1986 and was named Player of the Year for the second time a year later. He left the club after they were relegated following the play-off defeat to Middlesbrough. A tribunal set a £925,000 fee for his switch to Everton. Has an arts degree, was Motherwell's chief executive, now lives in the Borders and enjoys a successful career as television pundit and newspaper columnist.

*Photo: sueandandyj56*

## NEWTON, Eddie

*Appearances: 214 Goals: 10 (1990-1999) Career: Chelsea, Cardiff City, Birmingham City, Oxford United, Barnet. (1990-2000).* Newton made his way through the ranks at the club to become a regular in the midfield engine room. Was at his best at the base of a midfield diamond before the signing of Didier Deschamps and injuries took their toll on his stay with the club. Gave away a penalty in the 1994 FA Cup Final defeat at the hands of Manchester United and then netted the winner against Middlesbrough three years later. Left the club for Birmingham City on a free transfer after nine seasons service. Coached a kids school team before setting up his own business, New Vision Sports, as well as helping to coach the Chelsea youths. Has co-presented Football Icon on Sky and is now assistant head coach at WBA having previously worked with MK Dons.

## NICHOLAS, Brian

*Appearances: 29 Goals: 1 (1955-1958) Career: Queens Park Rangers, Chelsea, Coventry City. (1950-1962).* Signed from west London rivals QPR as first reserve to Ken Armstrong and found his chances few and far between. Then after Armstrong retired, John Mortimore was bought in and rather than play in the reserves anymore Nicholas left for Coventry City in a £3,000 deal. Has made Coventry his home and worked for many years until his retirement as a machine operator for Massey Ferguson, still attends home games at Coventry.

*Photo: Feggy*

## NICHOLAS, Peter

*Appearances: 93 Goals: 2 (1988-1991) Career: Crystal Palace, Arsenal, Crystal Palace, Luton Town, Chelsea, Watford (1977-1993).* An uncompromising defensive midfielder who was bought in along with Graham Roberts by Bobby Campbell for £350,000 in August 1988, to add extra bit and composure to midfield with immediate reward as the club cantered to a Second Division Championship, a decade after he first won the same title with Crystal Palace. Became only the second Chelsea skipper to lift a trophy at Wembley when the club won the Full Members Cup in 1990, but when Campbell decided that it was time to give youth a chance the following season he was sold to Watford for £175,000 aged 31. Welsh international coached the youth teams at Chelsea and Palace where he also became assistant manager, now back to Wales managing Barry Town, Newport and until 2009 Llanelli and then joined the Neath coaching staff.

## NICHOLAS, Tony

*Appearances: 63 Goals: 20 (1955-1960) Career: Chelsea, Brighton and Hove Albion, Leyton Orient. (1955-1966).* Having served his time on the Chelsea ground staff, this quick and agile inside forward had the misfortune to be around the club at the same time as Jimmy Greaves. He never lived up to his early promise after making his league debut as an 18 year-old when Ted Drake was looking to make wholesale changes to his aging squad that had won the Championship in 1955. Enjoyed his most productive spell in the autumn of 1957 when he scored six goals in nine games. The signing of Johnny Brooks spelled the end of his stay with the club and Brighton paid a club record £15,000 to take him to South Coast. He ran a successful DIY business after retiring from football. Died in September 2005.

## NICHOLLS, Mark

*Appearances: 52 Goals: 3 (1995-2001)*
*Career: Chelsea, Reading, Grimsby*
*Town, Colchester United, Aldershot Town,*
*Torquay United. (1995-2001).* Came
through the ranks at the club, but despite
being a regular in the squad for the 1996-
97 season, he remained on the fringes
and was pushed out altogether as the
number of foreign players at the club
increased. Did win a League Cup winners
medal in 1998 before joining Reading on
loan but a permanent deal fell through. He
spent two more years largely as a reserve
before being handed a free transfer.
Never really settled anywhere afterwards
and drifted into non-league football,
playing for a club a season. His last club
was Bedfont and he now works as a
leisure centre manager.

## NIEDZWIECKI, Eddie

*Appearances: 175 Goals: 0 (1983-1988)*
*Career: Wrexham, Chelsea. (1977-1987).*
John Neal returned to his former club
Wrexham to pay £45,000 for the
Welshmen born to Polish parents. Under
the guidance of Peter Bonetti, he quickly
established himself in the first team and
helped the club to the Second Division
Championship in his first season at
Stamford Bridge. Quick and agile, he
earned the nickname 'Steady Eddie' but
the start of downward spiral came when
he seriously damaged his knee against
QPR in March 1986. When he returned to
action again, it was clear that he had lost a
lot of his ability and after five operations
on the knee he was forced to retire early
in July 1988 with the club receiving an
insurance payout of £125,000. Ran his own
sportswear firm specialising in
goalkeepers' equipment then held
coaching positions with Chelsea, Reading,
Arsenal and Wales, before joining
Blackburn in September 2004. Followed
Mark Hughes to Man City until December
2009, he then had a spell at West Ham but
is now first-team coach at Fulham.

## NUTTON, Mickey

*Appearances: 83 Goals: 0 (1977-1983)*
*Career: Chelsea, Reading, Millwall. (1978-*
*1987).* Enjoyed several runs in the first
team without ever really establishing
himself as a regular, not least because of
the stiff competition that he faced from
Colin Pates and Gary Chivers. Nutton did
enjoy a decent partnership with Mickey
Droy whom he proved to be an ideal foil
for between 1979 and 1981, but after a
run of injuries it became clear that he was
never going to fully realise his potential.
George Graham returned to his former
club to take Nutton 'south of the river' to
Millwall for £65,000 in March 1983. Played
for non league side Fisher and Erith &
Belvedere. Continues to live in Crystal
Palace and works in the building industry.

## O'CONNELL, Seamus

*Appearances: 17 Goals: 12 (1954-1956)*
*Career: Middlesbrough, Chelsea, Carlisle*
*United. (1953-1957).* An amateur who only
played one season at Stamford Bridge but
picked up a League Championship
winners medal at the end of it (in 1955).
He scored a hat trick on his debut, which
ended in a 6-5 defeat to Manchester
United in October 1964 and in the end he
contributed seven goals towards the
cause during the march to the title. Moved
to Spain, where he became successful in
the cattle business. Had a stroke some
years ago and has suffered from ill health
ever since.

**Tribute to 'Ossie' on the Shed wall.**

## O'DOWD, Peter

*Appearances: 87 Goals: 0 (1931-1934)*
Career: *Blackburn Rovers, Burnley, Chelsea, Torquay United. (1926-1937).* One of the most prominent players during the 1930's, he arrived at the club for £5,250 when Chelsea took advantage of Burnley's financial plight to bring him south. He quickly became one of the best centre halfs that has ever played for the Blues. An intelligent player, his league debut ended in a heavy defeat to Everton when Dixie Dean scored five goals. He fell out with the club's management and in the end he became the first English player that a French club paid money for when Valenciennes parted with £3,000 to offer him greater financial rewards. He was forced to retire aged 29 after breaking his leg in a trial match. Later owned his own drapery business in Weybridge, Surrey. Sadly died in May 1964 aged 56.

## OLIVEIRA, Filipe

*Appearances: 8 Goals: 0 (2001-2005)*
Career: *Chelsea, Preston North End. (2001-2005).* Bought from FC Porto as a teenager for a fee reported to be around £500,000. Made his Premiership debut against Manchester City but could never establish himself as a first team regular and was only able to make a handful of appearances. He had loan spells at Preston and then in his native Portugal with Maritimo before being released on a free transfer. Has played for Maritimo, Leixoes SC and since 2008 Braga.

## ORD, Tommy

*Appearances: 3 Goals: 1 (1972-1974)*
Career: *Chelsea, Bristol City. (1972-1974).* A hard working midfielder who despite financial problems causing player sales, was given a chance in the first team and he scored on his debut against Stoke City. Moved to the States to play for a number of NASL and Indoor teams, but has since returned to London and lives in the north of the capital.

## O'ROURKE, John

*Appearances: 1 Goals: 0 (1962-1963)*
Career: *Arsenal, Chelsea, Luton Town, Middlesbrough, Ipswich Town, Coventry City, Queens Park Rangers, Bournemouth, (1962-1974).* Moved to Stamford Bridge after an unsuccessful stint at Arsenal. Was top scorer for the reserves but couldn't make an impression on the first team where Graham Moore and Barry Bridges were near automatic choices. At the end of his career he stayed in Bournemouth, where he ran a newsagents.

## OSGOOD, Peter

*Appearances: 380 Goals: 150 (1964-1974 and 1978-1979)* Career: *Chelsea, Southampton, Norwich City, Chelsea. (1964-1979).* Windsor born 'Ossie' reached god like status at Stamford Bridge. He forced his way into the first team after scoring 30 goals in 20 reserve team outings, and duly delivered two goals in a League Cup tie at Workington in December 1964 on his debut. He became a regular thereafter but suffered a share of heartbreak along the way, missing the 1967 FA Cup Final as a result of a broken leg. Three years later he joined an elite band of players to score in every round of the competition including the final, he was also in target in the Cup Winners Cup Final victory over Real Madrid and the League Cup Final. He fell out with Dave Sexton and after being dropped and transfer listed, Southampton paid a club record £275,000 to take him to the South Coast. 'Ossie' returned to 'The Bridge' for one last stand but the club were in decline and he retired in September 1979 to run the Union Inn in Windsor. Later turned his hand to sports promotion and was youth team coach at Portsmouth. Was a very popular after dinner speaker; match day host at Chelsea as well as television pundit until his death in March 2006 aged 59 following a heart attack at a family funeral. His Ashes were laid to rest underneath the penalty spot at Shed End.

*Photo: artefatte*

## PANNUCCI, Christian

*Appearances 10 Goals: 1 (2000)*
Career: *Chelsea (2000)*. Italian defender who was brought to the club by Gianluca Vialli with Albert Ferrer injured and Dan Petrescu departed. He settled in well, but as soon as Claudio Ranieri came to the club, his days were numbered and he going back to Milan. Joined Monaco briefly before returning to Italy with Roma and then Parma until January 2010 when his contract was terminated after seven months at the club.

## PARSONS, Eric

*Appearances: 177 Goals: 42 (1950-1956)*
Career: *West Ham United, Chelsea, Brentford. (1947-1961)*. The former 'Desert Rat' who served in Montgomery's Eighth Army during the Second World, war was purchased for £23,000 in November 1950, a huge amount at the time. Nicknamed 'the Rabbit' due to his lightening speed, he was an outside right, who could be rated alongside the likes of Tom Finney and Stanley Matthews. However, their presence in the League at the same time also restricted his international honours to one England 'B' cap. As well as being the main provider for Roy Bentley during the 1955 Championship winning success, he also chipped in with more than his fair share including two against Sheffield Wednesday to secure the title. Commuted from his native Worthing while playing for the club along with Stan Willemse and Johnny McNichol. He still lives in the town in retirement, having run a successful sign writing business. Previously he had also owned a grocery shop and a cigarette vending business.

**Paul Parker and Graham Roberts.** *Photo: Lancs & Cheshire Amateur Football League*

## PARKER, Paul

*Appearances: 4  Goals: 0 (1997)*
*Career: Fulham, QPR, Man United, Derby County, Sheff United, Fulham, Chelsea. (1982-1997).* Signed for the club in the middle of an injury crisis but only started one game before being released. Became director of football at non-league Ashford Town, then managed Chelmsford and Welling United before going into pundit work with Setanta. Is now an ambassador for the Blue Square League.

*Photo: Rod George*

## PATES, Colin

*Appearances: 346  Goals: 10 (1979-1988)*
*Career: Chelsea, Charlton Athletic, Arsenal, Brighton, (1979-1994).* Colin made his debut in the 7-3 win over Leyton Orient in November 1979. Over the next couple of seasons, he had plenty of chances, given Micky Droy's injury problems, but it wasn't until John Neal was appointed manager that he nailed down a regular start. Along with Joe McLaughlin, formed the bedrock foundations on which the 1984 Second Division Championship

side was built and then the Full Members Cup Final victory two seasons later. It was assumed that he would be a one club man and there was some dismay when it was announced that Bobby Campbell had sold him to Charlton Athletic for £430,000. Had a spell at Crawley before coaching at the Arsenal School of Excellence, but since 2001 he has coached football at Whitgift School in South Croydon.

## PATON, John

*Appearances: 23  Goals: 3 (1946-1947)*
*Career: Chelsea, Brentford, Watford. (1946-1955).* A press photographer by profession, he had played in the same RAF team during the War as Stanley Matthews. However, his stay at Chelsea was to be a short one, he left just seven months after moving from Celtic for £10,000 in November 1946. By the end of the season he had returned to Parkhead. Managed Watford for a spell before spending six years at Arsenal as a scout and then 'A' team coach. He was also in charge of Herts FA's youth coaching scheme before taking over the management of a snooker hall. There he became a professional coach and referee. Now lives in retirement in London.

## PAYNE, Joe

*Appearances: 47  Goals: 23 (1938-1946)*
*Career: Luton Town, Chelsea, West Ham United, Millwall. (1934-1948).* Arrived at the Stamford Bridge for a bargain £5,000 in 1938 but had the had the misfortune of seeing his time at the club truncated by the outbreak of World War 2, indeed he scored in the each of the last six games before the war. Served in the RAF as Sergeant Payne and played in the 1944 and 1945 South League Cup Finals. Suffered from injuries towards the end of his stay at the club and was sent to West Ham in a player swap with Harry Medhurst. Probably best known for scoring 10 goals in a game for Luton. Died in Luton April 1975 aged 61.

## PEACOCK, Gavin

*Appearances: 134 Goals: 27 (1993-1996)*
Career: *Queens Park Rangers, Gillingham, Bournemouth, Newcastle United, Chelsea, Queens Park Rangers, Charlton Athletic. (1984-2002).* Joined the Blues for £1.25 million from Newcastle United in August 1993 after he fell out with the club's management at St James's Park. The investment proved to be money well spent, a willing worker, he hit the crossbar from 25 yards in the 1994 FA Cup Final and finished joint top scorer with 14 goals in the same season, to prove his usefulness in front of goal. Returned to one of his previous clubs, QPR, for £1million in 1996 after losing his place to Roberto Di Matteo. Ended his playing career at Charlton Athletic in 2001 and became a pundit with the BBC. He decided to quit the role and dedicate more time to religion with view to becoming a Christian minister. This prompted a move to Canada to take a three-year masters course in Divinity at Ambrose Seminary. Now lives with his family in the Rocky Mountains having already studied theology at Ridley Hall, Cambridge.

## PEARCE, Ian

*Appearances: 5 Goals: 0 (1991-1993)*
Career: *Chelsea, Blackburn Rovers, West Ham United, Fulham, Southampton, Lincoln City. (1990-2010).* Will always be seen as 'one who got away'. Only made five sub appearances for the club after making his debut against Liverpool in May 1992. He was sold to Blackburn Rovers for £300,000 the following October. Is now player assistant manager of Lincoln City after previously played non league football for Kingstonian.

## PERCASSI, Luca

*Appearances: 2 Goals: 0 (1998-2000)*
Career: *Chelsea. (1998-2000).* Percassi was signed from Atalanta as a 17 year-old along with team mate Sam Della Bona but never made the grade. While at the club, he only make two substitute appearances before leaving for Monza on a free transfer. Quit professional football in 2004 to become an entrepreneur in Italy, but then in June 2010 his father bought his first club, Atalanta, and installed Luca as general manager.

## PETIT, Emmanuel

*Appearances: 76 Goals: 3 (2001-2004)*
Career: *Arsenal, Chelsea. (1997-2004).* Signed for £7.5 million in the summer of 2001 after seeing off competition from Manchester United and Tottenham Hotspur. He largely struggled in his first season at the club but still managed to play in the 2002 FA Cup Final defeat to his former club. Vastly improved in his second season and impressed in midfield alongside Frank Lampard, helping the club to finish in fourth place in the Premiership. A series of knee injuries halted his progress and he was one of the first players to be axed by Jose Mourinho when he arrived at the club. Guest starred in the Christmas episode of the Bill and has worked as a television pundit in France. Also an ambassador for Barclays Spaces for Sport.

## PETRESCU, Dan

*Appearances: 208  Goals: 23 (1995-2000)*
Career: *Sheffield Wednesday, Chelsea, Bradford City, Southampton. (1994-2002).* A Romanian international who was part of the Blues' successes in the 1997 FA Cup and the 1998 League Cup and Cup Winners Cup teams. Petrescu left two years later after falling out with Gianluca Vialli following a defeat to Manchester United and was never to play for the club again. He even failed to make the subs bench for the 2000 FA Cup Final and was sold to Bradford City for £1 million. Has managed clubs in Romanian, Poland and now Russian First division club Kuban Krasnodar since December 2009.

*Photo: Dan Avraham*

## PEYTON, Gerry

*Appearances: 1  Goals: 0 (1993)*
Career: *Burnley, Fulham, Southend United, Bournemouth, Everton, Bolton Wanderers, Norwich City, Brentford, Chelsea, West Ham United. (1975-1994).* The Republic of Ireland international was signed on loan as cover for Dmitri Kharine and made his only appearance as a sub for the Russian in a 2-0 defeat at the hands of Sheffield Wednesday. Is now the Arsenal goalkeeping coach having previously coached in Japan and Sweden as well as Bournemouth, Birmingham city and West Brom.

## PHELAN, Terry

*Appearances: 24  Goals: 0 (1995-1996)*
Career: *Leeds United, Swansea City, Wimbledon, Manchester City, Chelsea, Everton, Crystal Palace, Fulham, Sheffield United. (1984-2001).* A vastly experienced left back when he was signed for £900,000 in November 1995 after Scott Minto suffered an injury. He arrived at the club with a hamstring injury which checked his progress during his two seasons at Stamford Bridge. This meant that he was only ever really around the fringes of the first team squad and was sold to Everton for £850,000 in January 1997. Now lives in New Zealand where he coached Otago United. Spends his summer teaching youth soccer at One on One Soccer while working as football development manager for Football South. Lives in McAndrew Bay, Dunedin.

## PHILLIPS, John

*Appearances: 149  Goals: 0 (1970-1980)*
Career: *Shrewsbury Town, Aston Villa, Chelsea, Crewe Alexandra, Brighton., Charlton Athletic, Crystal Palace (1968-1983).* A £30,000 capture from Aston Villa when future Villa keeper Tommy Hughes broke his leg. As understudy to Peter Bonetti, he still managed to rack up 150 appearances during his decade at Stamford Bridge. He played a key role in reaching the 1971 Cup Winners' Cup Final, playing in both legs in the third round and semi final even though 'The Cat' returned to face Real Madrid. The Welsh international was eventually sold to Brighton for £15,000. Continues to run the motor factors company that he set up in Mitcham while still playing for Crystal Palace. Both his father and grandfather played League football.

### PICKERING, Peter

*Appearances: 35 Goals: 0 (1948-1951)*
*Career: York City, Chelsea, Northampton
Tow. (1946-1955).* The club paid a then
record £20,000 to bring Pickering to the
club in 1948. He shared goalkeeping
duties with Harry Medhurst and played 19
games in his first season. Struggled to
overcome inconsistency and was sold in
June 1951 to Kettering Town for £250. He
later emigrated to South Africa, where he
became a first class cricket umpire. Lived
in the Cape Town area and worked for
Columbit who manufactured heavy duty
kitchenware. He then joined Jack Lemkus
Sports before assisting in the sports
department of Hensilwoods. Died in
November 2006.

### PINNER, Mike

*Appearances: 1 Goals: 0 (1961-1962)*
*Career: Aston Villa, Sheffield Wednesday,
Queens Park Rangers, Manchester
United, Chelsea, Arsenal, Chelsea,
Swansea City, Leyton Orient. (1954-1965).*
One of the leading amateur goalkeepers
of his era, had two mini spells at Stamford
Bridge in the same season. Made one
start for the club when Peter Bonetti and
his understudy Errol McNally were both
injured in April 1962. Worked as a solicitor
for most his career, played in two Olympic
Games, and was still working for the
London law firm Michael Hatchick
Solicitors well into his 70's.

### PLUM, Seth

*Appearances: 27 Goals: 1 (1924-1926)*
*Career: Charlton Athletic, Chelsea,
Southend United. (1922-1927).* An
England international wing half who spent
most of his time at the club in the
reserves. Found his first team chances few
and far between, even though when given
a chance he didn't let anyone down. Lived
in his native north London and worked as
a petrol pump attendant. He died in St
Annes Hospital, Tottenham in November
1969 aged 70.

Photo: Mark Page

### POYET, Gustavo

*Appearances: 145 Goals: 49 (1997-2001)*
*Career: Chelsea, Tottenham Hotspur,
Swindon Town. (1997-2006).* An attacking
midfielder who was signed on a free
transfer from Real Zaragoza and went onto
to give the club four years excellent
service. He suffered a cruciate knee
ligament injury not long after his arrival
but returned in time to help secure the
Cup Winners Cup. His second season saw
a return of 14 goals, one of which was the
winner in the Super Cup Final. His third
piece of silverware came in the shape of
the FA Cup. He continued the run with
victory in the Charity Shield before the
arrival of Claudio Ranieri saw him fall out
of favour, request a transfer and move to
Spurs for £2.2million. Worked under
Dennis Wise at Swindon Town and Leeds.
He was then Juande Ramos's assistant at
Spurs. Poyet has been manager of
Brighton since November 2009.

**GUESS WHO? - see page 150 for answers.** *Photo: Rowan Farnham-Long*

## POTRAC, Tony

*Appearances: 1  Goals: 0 (1970-1973)*
Career: *Chelsea. (1970-1973).* Spent a
total of five years at the club, only making
one appearance, in a 2-2 draw with
Huddersfield Town in January 1972,
replacing Chris Garland. He may have
been unfortunate to have been registered
at a time of savage financial cuts and was
one of many players released without
making a first team break-through. He
moved to South African club Durban City
but is now back in the UK and living in
Bexley, Kent.

## PRIESTLEY, Peter

*Appearances: 23  Goals: 0 (1933-1934)*
Career: *Chelsea. (1933-1934).* May be
best remembered for wearing a rugby
style skull cap to hide his premature
balding. Chelsea held off competition
from several leading clubs to sign their
man for £2,000 from Linfield in 1933. Mud
in the eye caused a major injury and he
returned to Ireland after only one season
in London. The club retained his
registration for several years before he
finally announced his retirement. He
became a school principal in Lambeth,
but died suddenly following an operation
at the Royal Victoria Hospital in July 1985
aged 74.

## PROUDFOOT, Peter

*Appearances: 12  Goals: 0 (1906-1907)*
Career: *Lincoln City, Millwall, Clapton
Orient, Chelsea, Stockport County. (1900-
1913).* A hard tackling wing half was
signed for £120 from financially stricken
Orient. He made his debut against
Manchester United in April 1906 in front of
67,000 but he was never able to hold
down a first team place. Earned a
commission during the Great War, had
three spells as Orient manager before
retiring through ill health in 1939.
Proudfoot then returned to his native
Wishaw where he died in March 1941
aged 59.

Photo: Steindy

## QUARESMA, Ricardo

*Appearances: 4  Goals: 0 (2009)*
Career: *Sporting CP, Barcelona, Porto,
Internazionale, Chelsea (loan), Besiktas
(2001-2010.* Portuguese defender who
played four games on loan from Inter in
2009. Now playing for Turkish side
Besiktas following a £6 million transfer in
June 2010.

## RANDALL, Ernie

*Appearances: 3  Goals: 1 (1950-1953)*
Career: *Chelsea, Crystal Palace. (1950-
1955).* He enjoyed a rapid rise from non
league Bognor Regis Town to the first
division. Made his debut against WBA in
October 1951 replacing Bobby Smith and
scored his only goal against Aston Villa in
a 2-2 draw in the same season. Despite
being a regular scorer for the reserves
and 'A' team he had Roy Bentley as
competition and slowly drifted back into
obscurity. After hanging up his boots, he
went to work for British Rail in Redhill and
then London Waterloo before retiring.

# RANKIN, John

*Appearances: 66 Goals: 9 (1930-1934)*
Career: *Doncaster Rovers, Charlton Athletic, Chelsea, Notts County. (1924-1936).* He was signed for £3,000 in May 1930 but he never quite settled in the team. Despite having two long runs in successive seasons he was allowed to join Notts County in 1934. Returned North of the Border where he became a Glasgow greengrocer, he died in 1989.

# RHOADES-BROWN, Peter

*Appearances: 109 Goals: 5 (1979-1984)*
Career: *Chelsea, Oxford United. (1979-1988).* Joined the club as a schoolboy before making his way through the ranks. A classy performer with pace and close control, made the left flank his own between 1981 and 1983. Is best remembered for a goal he scored against Liverpool in the FA Cup, picking up a ball on the halfway line before slotting past Bruce Grobbelaar. Was sold to Oxford United for £75,000 and is still working for the same club, heading their community programme, having previously worked in the commercial office.

Photo: Rod George

# RICHARDSON, Fred

*Appearances: 2 Goals: 0 (1946-1947)*
Career: *Chelsea, Hartlepool United, Barnsley, WBA, Chester City, Hartlepool United. (1946-1956).* A centre forward who was largely kept in the reserves by the legendary Tommy Lawton. Only made two first team appearances, with his debut coming in a defeat against Everton in April 1947. Became a scout for WBA in the North East and coached several clubs in the Hartlepool area. Managed Whickham to their FA Vase success in 1981. Now lives in retirement in the North East.

# RIX, Graham

*Appearances: 4 Goals: 0 (1994-1995)*
Career: *Arsenal, Brentford, Chelsea. (1975-1995).* Joined the club as a non contract player and youth team coach but was pressed into action, becoming the club's oldest debutant in a Cup Winners' Cup tie against Viktoria Zizkov in September 1994. He officially retired at the end of the same season but stayed on at the club and became assistant manager to Ruud Gullit and then Gianluca Vialli. Served six months in prison for having under-age sex with a minor, but returned to the club and was appointed caretaker boss following Vialli's departure. Also had spells in charge of Oxford United and Portsmouth but is now a coach at the Glenn Hoddle Academy in Southern Spain.

## ROBBEN, Arjen

*Appearances: 67  Goals: 15 (2004-2007)*
*Career: Groningen, PSV, Chelsea, Real Madrid, Bayern Munich (2000-2010.* One the stars of the 2010 World Cup, Robben signed for Bayern Munich in August 2009 in a deal worth about £22 million.

## ROBERTS, Graham

*Appearances: 83  Goals: 22 (1988-1990)*
*Career: Portsmouth, Tottenham, Chelsea, West Bromwich Albion. (1977-1993).* A born leader,  Roberts was worth every penny of the £475,000 spent to tempt him from Rangers. An aggressive player who never gave an inch whose 12 penalties were a major bonus when the club romped to the Second Division title. Was appointed to the coaching staff by Bobby Campbell but left the club following a row with Ken Bates. He has managed Yeovil and Clyde in Scotland has since worked as a media pundit for the likes of Sky and Talksport.

*Photo: The Prostate Cancer Charity*

**Arjen Robben.** *Photo: Steffe*

## ROBERTSON, Bill G

*Appearances: 215 Goals: 0 (1946-1960)*
Career: *Chelsea, Leyton Orient. (1950-1962)*. Robertson couldn't have come into the team at a worse time, 14 successive defeats and four points adrift at the foot of the table the drop was a near certainly. He produced an inspired display on his debut at Liverpool, this combined with a four match unbeaten run saw the club avoid relegation by the narrowest of margins. It also secured him his place, which he kept for the next season six seasons including the 1955 Championship winning campaign. He lost his spot to Reg Matthews and returned to the reserves. Sadly passed away in Tadworth in 1973 aged only 45. He was the owner of a pub when he suffered a fatal heart attack.

## ROBERTSON, Bill H

*Appearances: 43 Goals: 0 (1945-1948)*
Career: *Chelsea, Birmingham City, Stoke City. (1945-1960)*. Signed to replace the legendary Vic Woodley but had to share duties with Harry Medhurst for two seasons before joining Birmingham in November 1948 for £2,500. Ran his own newsagents in Stoke on Trent before returning to his native Berkshire where he died in 1973 aged 50.

## ROBERTSON, John Tait

*Appearances: 39 Goals: 4 (1905-1906)*
Career: *Everton, Southampton, Chelsea, Glossop North End. (1895-1909)*. Earned his place in club history for not only being their first manager (as well as player) on a salary of £4 a week, but also for scoring their first league goal against Blackpool in September 1905. He assembled a good side but suddenly left the club for Glossop North End in January 1906 with the club third in the Second Division table. Stayed at Glossop until becoming reserve team manager of Manchester United. Coached on the continent either side of WW1 and became trainer of Coventry City before his death in Hampshire in January 1935.

## ROBINSON, Arthur

*Appearances: 3 Goals: 0 (1908-1910)*
Career: *Birmingham City, Chelsea, Coventry City. (1898-1911)*. Was signed as cover for Jack Whitley and is said to have always worn two goalkeeping jerseys whatever the weather. Also only wore two pairs as boots throughout his career according to legend. Found his chances at Stamford Bridge hard to come by and moved on to Coventry City in 1910. Settled in the city where he became licensee of the Red Lion Inn, Barrass Green. Died in May 1929 aged 51.

## ROBSON, Bryan 'Pop'

*Appearances: 17 Goals: 5 (1982-1983)*
Career: *Newcastle United, West Ham United, Sunderland, West Ham United, Sunderland, Carlisle United, Chelsea, Carlisle United, Sunderland, Carlisle United. (1964-1985)*. Joined the club when he was almost 37 and clearly well past his best. He still managed to score on his debut against Cambridge in August 1982, but it was never going to be a long term signing by John Neal and he left for Sunderland after just one season at Stamford Bridge. Managed Sunderland and Carlisle, coached at Manchester United, Hartlepool, Leeds, has been the community coach at Sunderland also scouted for Birmingham. Now runs his own newsagents in Hexham.

## ROBSON, Tom

*Appearances: 7 Goals: 0 (1965-1966)*
Career: *Northampton Town, Chelsea, Newcastle United, Peterborough United. (1961-1980)*. Signed from Northampton Town for £30,000 in December 1965. Found his chances at the club limited because of Bobby Tambling, and within 12 months he was on his way to Newcastle United for just £13,000. Settled in Peterborough after playing 450 games for them and became Property Manager for a local newspaper.

## ROCASTLE, David

*Appearances: 40  Goals: 2 (1994-1998)*
Career: *Arsenal, Leeds United, Manchester City, Chelsea, Norwich City, Hull City. (1984-1998).* He had clearly seen better days when he arrived at the club for £1.25 million. Was given a regular berth on the right hand side of midfield whereas he would probably have preferred to have played in the middle of the park. His second season was wrecked by a broken toe and despite two spells out on loan he was unable to regain his first team place. Was left to see out the last two years of his contract in the reserves. Later played for Norwich City and Hull City. Rocky sadly died in March 2001 aged 33, two months after being diagnosed as suffering from non-Hodgkin's lymphoma. He is one of 16 Arsenal legends to have their images painted on the side of the Emirates Stadium.

## ROFE, Dennis

*Appearances: 63  Goals: 0 (1980-1982)*
Career: *Leyton Orient, Leicester City, Chelsea, Southampton. (1967-1983).* Signed by Geoff Hurst for £80,000 when he needed to inject some experience and professionalism into his squad. Despite taking his time to settle into the squad, faith in the former England Under 23 international was repaid with a run of 54 consecutive appearances. Was appointed captain by Hurst for a spell in the 1980-81 season but his run in the side came to an end through a groin injury and he lost his place to Chris Hutchings. This ultimately resulted in him being given a free transfer and joining Southampton in July 1982. Had spells coaching Bristol Rovers (who he managed briefly), Stoke City, Kingstonian and Fulham, sandwiched in between long stints at Saints, which finally ended in 2005. Rofe has since worked for BBC radio, the Premier League in the Bahamas and for the Football League as a regional development officer.

## ROUGVIE, Doug

*Appearances:100  Goals:3 (1984-1987)*
Career: *Chelsea, Brighton, Shrewsbury Town, Fulham, (1974-1988).* A hard tackling, no nonsense left back who often bordered on the reckless. He arrived in a £150,000 deal to replace Joey Jones and wasted no time in making his mark with a crunching challenge on Arsenal's Viv Anderson on his debut. Quickly became a regular in the side but a lack of pace hampered his progress and he was unfortunate enough to score an own goal in the Full Members Cup victory over Manchester City at Wembley. He was sold to Shrewsbury Town in the summer of 1987 for £73,000 after it became clear that he wasn't going to play any part in John Hollins long term plans. A tough Scottish international defender, Rougvie now lives in the Aberdeen area and works in engineering after running his own design company.

## SAUNDERS, Derek

*Appearances: 223  Goals: 9 (1953-1958)*
Career: *Chelsea (1953-1958).* Saunders was working as a shipping clerk near Stamford Bridge when he was persuaded by Ted Drake to join the professional ranks, after previously playing for Walthamstow Avenue. A highly skilled wing half, he formed a fearsome barrier with Stan Willemse. An ever present in the 1955 Championship winning side, he was appointed team captain in 1957 to help the steady influx after youngsters Drake's Ducklings. He announced his retirement a couple of years later following a stint out with injury. Joined the club's coaching staff, then worked as groundsman and chief soccer coach at Westminster School before becoming groundsman at Hampstead Cricket Club. Was also tutor-in-charge of Putney and Wandsworth Adult Education under the Inner London Authority. Now lives in retirement in Frinton on Sea, Essex.

**GUESS WHO? - see page 150 for answers.** *Photo: Rod George*

## SCOTT, Mel

*Appearances:104  Goals:0 (1956-1963)*
Career: *Chelsea, Brentford. (1956-1967).*
A product of the clubs prolific youth
system but never really fulfiled his
potential despite playing over 100 games
for the club. A solid centre half, he made
his debut against Wolves in March 1958,
but a lack of domination in the air against
big centre forwards cost him his place in
the team when John Mortimore was
moved into the middle at the back after
the arrival of Sylvan Anderson. Died of a
heart attack in 1997 whilst living in the US
where he ended his career.

## SHARP, Jimmy

*Appearances:64  Goals:0 (1912-1915)*
Career: *Fulham, Arsenal, Fulham,
Chelsea, Fulham. (1904-1920).* The
former miner moved to Stamford Bridge
for £1,750 in November 1912 after
spending a few months in the USA. He
took over from Jock Cameron and did
very well for two seasons before losing his
place to Jack Harrow. His career was
ended by the outbreak of the First World
War, except for one game, while on the
Fulham coaching staff,when a player
missed the bus. Coached at Fulham,
Walsall and Cliftonville, then went into the
building trade in London in the 1930's. He
died in November 1949 aged 69.

## SHAW, Colin

*Appearances: 1  Goals:0 (1961-1963)*
Career: *Chelsea, Norwich City, Leyton
Orient. (1960-1966).* Despite an
impressive scoring record for the juniors
and reserves, he never cut it at first team
level. Once scored seven goals in an FA
Youth Cup tie with Fulham. Only made
one first team appearance, standing in for
Barry Bridges in a defeat against West
Ham United in February 1962. Was sold to
Norwich City for £3,500 but has lived in
South Africa since 1966. Was managing
director of a Hi-Tec sports distributor in
Johannesburg.

## SHEARER, Duncan

*Appearances: 2  Goals: 1 (1983-1986)*
Career: *Chelsea, Huddersfield Town,
Swindon Town, Blackburn Rovers. (1983-
1992).* Failed to get a look in at the
Stamford Bridge because of the fruitful
Kerry Dixon/David Speedie partnership.
However he did score on his debut
against Leicester in February 1986 and
played against Oxford the following week,
in two of the three games Dixon didn't
play that season. He was allowed to leave
the club to join Huddersfield in a £100,000
deal in March 1986. Ended his career in
Scotland with Aberdeen and then
Inverness Caledonian Thistle. Joined the
coaching staff of both clubs before taking
control of Buckie Thistle for four and a half
years. Shearer is now coaching the under
15's at Inverness and working for the
Press Association in Scotland.

## SHEERIN, Joe

*Appearances: 1  Goals:0 (1996-2000)*
Career: *Chelsea, Bournemouth. (1996-
2000).* Had the shortest Premier League
career on record after making his only
appearance in the closing moments of a
win away to Wimbledon in April 1997 as a
substitute for Giafranco Zola. He left the
Blues in February 2002. Has played for
Croydon Athletic, Kingstonian, AFC
Wimbledon and Leatherhead since 2006.

Photo: -AX-

**S**

## SHELITTO, Ken

*Appearances: 123 Goals: 2 (1959-1969)*
Career: *Chelsea. (1959-1969)*. A member of Chelsea's FA Youth Cup winning squad in 1958, he made his league debut against Nottingham Forest a season later but had to wait for Ted Drake to leave to get a regular chance as part of Tommy Docherty's remodelled side. Helped win promotion from Division Two in 1963 and was pencilled in to be part of Sir Alf Ramsey's World Cup plans until he suffered a serious knee injury. After several failed fitness attempts, he had to quit at the age of 28. Joined the coaching staff as youth team coach and then as youth team manager before stepping up in July 1977 to manage the first team. With the team struggling near the bottom of the First Division, he resigned in December 1978 to end 23 years service. Is now a permanent resident of Malaysia and has been a technical analyst for the Asian Football Confederation. Also worked for QPR, Crystal Palace, Preston and Wolves before heading to the Far East.

## SHERWOOD, Steve

*Appearances: 17 Goals:0 (1971-1976)*
Career: *Chelsea, Millwall, Brentford, Watford, Grimsby Town (1971-1994)*. Spotted while playing in West Riding and made his debut against Derby in December 1971. He only arrived at the ground five minutes before kick off after answering an emergency SOS when it was discovered that both Peter Bonetti and John Phillips were injured. He eventually became first choice in the 1975-76 season, but after some unsteady displays, Eddie McCreadie replaced him with Bonetti who had rejoined the club. The brother of John Sherwood, who won an Olympic 400m hurdles bronze medal in 1968, he headed Grimsby youth set up before becoming an independent financial adviser in Lincolnshire. He is now working in office management and still living in the same area.

**Andriy Shevchenko**

## SHEVCHENKO, Andriy

*Appearances: 47 Goals: 9 (2006-2009)*
Career: *Dynamo Kiev, AC Milan, Chelsea, AC Milan, Dynamo Kiev (1994-2010)*. Returned home to first club Dynamo Kiev on 28th August 2009.

## SHIPPERLEY, Neil

*Appearances: 48 Goals: 9 (1992-1995)*
Career: *Chelsea, Watford, Southampton, Crystal Palace, Barnsley, Wimbledon, Crystal Palace, Sheffield United, Brentford. (1992-2007)*. Signed for the Blues after leaving school and was a prolific marksman for the youth and reserve teams before enjoying a rapid rise to fame. Dave Webb gave him his first team debut and he netted on his first start against Wimbledon. However, he had to wait until Glenn Hoddle took over as manager for another run, but the signings of Mark Stein and then Paul Furlong signalled that despite his promise he was never going to stay at the club. Alan Ball paid a club record £1.25 million to take him to Southampton. Went into non league management with Bedfont FC and from June 2010, Walton Casuals.

Photo: Joe Gazman

## SIDWELL, Steve

*Appearances: 15 Goals: 0 (2007-2008)*
Career: *Arsenal, Brentford, Beveren, Brighton, Reading, Chelsea, Aston Villa (1999-2010).* Joined Aston Villa in July 2008.

## SILLETT, John

*Appearances:102 Goals:1 (1953-1962)*
Career: *Chelsea, Coventry City, Plymouth Argyle. (1953-1962).* Brother of Peter, was a full back who gave nothing away. Signed after doing his national service. Made his league debut against Manchester United on New Years Day 1957 but he had to wait until the start of the 1958-59 season to become a first team regular, partnering his bother on the flanks for three seasons until he lost his place to Ken Shellito. Then left to start a love affair with Coventry City, which included winning the FA Cup as manager. Was chief scout for Portsmouth and then worked for Central Television and did some scouting for Sven Goran Eriksson but is now retired.

## SILLETT, Peter

Career: *Southampton, Chelsea (1951-1961).* Ted Drake had to persuade Sillett's mother to let him make the £13,000 move from Southampton in the summer 1953 and he had to take his brother John as part of the deal. A committed and determined player, he lacked pace but was a member of the 1955 Championship winning side sharing the right back spot with John Harris. His penalty against Wolves virtually wrapped up the title. He was a regular in the side until his career was ended at the age of 30 by a broken leg. Earned more money with Guildford City than he did at Stamford Bridge despite being an England international. Managed a number of clubs around Kent and Sussex and scouted for his brother John when he was manager of Hereford and Coventry. An arthritic knee kept him housebound at his Ashford, home until his death in March 1998, aged 65 after a battle with cancer .

## SINCLAIR, Frank

*Appearances: 218 Goals: 13 (1990-1998)*
Career: *Chelsea, WBA, Leicester City, Burnley, Huddersfield Town, Lincoln City, Wycombe Wanderers. (1990-2009).* The Jamaican international gave excellent service during the eight seasons that he spent in the first team filling a verity of defensive roles. Was given his league debut at left back by Bobby Campbell as a 19 year-old against Luton Town despite being right footed. It wasn't until Paul Elliott's injury that he became established in central defence. He gave away a penalty in the 1994 FA Cup but then picked up a winner's medal three years later. He scored in the 1998 League Cup Final but found himself out in the cold when Gianluca Vialli started filling his side with foreign imports and was sold to Leicester for £2 million. Is currently playing for Wrexham in the Blue Square Premier.

## SISSONS, John

*Appearances: Goals: (1974-1975)*
*Career: West Ham United, Sheffield*
*Wednesday, Norwich City, Chelsea*
*(1962-1975).* Dave Sexton's last major signing for the club, when he was recruited for £70,000 from Norwich City in August 1974. The left winger had clearly seen better days and he struggled to make a impact. Despite starting the first ten games of the season, he found himself out in the cold as soon as Sexton departed the club and only made three more appearances before his contract was cancelled, seven months after he arrived. Became the youngest player to score in a Cup Final in 1963 and now lives in Cape Town, South Africa where he is a partner in a successful motor products and warranty firm.

## SITTON, John

*Appearances: Goals: (1977-1980)*
*Career: Chelsea, Millwall, Gillingham,*
*Leyton Orient (1978-1990).* Came through the ranks at the club but was mainly a reserve team player. He was given a run of games towards the end of the 1978-79 season when the club were already doomed to relegation but it was clear that he wasn't part of Geoff Hurst's long term plans and he was sold to Millwall for £2,000. As manager of Leyton Orient he sacked a player Terry Howard at half time of a game against Blackpool. Is now a black taxi driver, has worked for the FA on their coach education scheme and complied stats for the Press Association.

## SMEE, Roger

*Appearances: 0 Goals:0 (1966-1967)*
*Career: Chelsea, Reading, (1966-1973).*
Was a junior at Stamford Bridge but left the club for Reading without making a first team appearance. Went onto to become chairman of the Royals. Lives in Crazies Hill and is property tycoon owner of Rock Investment Group.

Photo: Comrad Fomin

## SMERTIN, Alexei

*Appearances: 25 Goals: 1 (2003-2006)*
*Career: Chelsea, Portsmouth, Charlton*
*Athletic, Fulham. (2003-2008).* Claudio Ranieri bought the Russian from French club Bordeaux in August 2003 for £3.45 million but then immediately sent him out on loan to Portsmouth for the season. When he returned to Stamford Bridge, new boss Jose Mourinho gave him a run in the team for the first third of the season but then reduced him to a bit part player. This was still enough to earn him a Championship winner's medal before leaving the club. In January 2006 he was sold to Dynamo Moscow for £1 million, but his stay in his homeland lasted less than a year when he returned to the capital to sign for Fulham. He played 22 games for the Cottagers but lost his place to Danny Murphy and decided to go into politics in his native Russia. In March 2009 was elected as an MP for the Altai region of Russia. It was announced in February 2010 that the former Russian captain had been appointed sports director in the country's bid to land either the 2018 or 2022 World Cup finals.

## SMETHURST, Derek

*Appearances: Goals: (1968-1971)*
*Career: Chelsea, Millwall (1968-1974)..*
Signed by Dave Sexton as a permit player when he left university in December 1968 and spent two seasons in the reserves. Having proved to be an able back up to Peter Osgood and Ian Hutchinson, he signed a professional deal in January 1971 after he completed a two year residency requirement. Played his part in the Cup Winners' Cup Final success later that season but was surprisingly sold to Millwall the following September for £35,000. Now involved with Youth Soccer in Florida and runs his own academy. Is a born again Christian after experiencing a vision whilst watching television in San Diego in 1978. Has a daughter called Chelsea!

## SMITH, Arthur

*Appearances: 49 Goals: 0 (1938-1945)*
*Career: Wolves, Bristol Rovers, Swindon Town, Chelsea. (1930-1945).* A left back who was signed from third division Swindon Town in March 1938 for £4,000. Thrust straight into the first team and not looking out of place, he looked set for a long stay in the side until the outbreak of World War Two stopped his progress. A broken leg in a car accident in 1945 ended his a career. Became Wolves

trainer before being appointed West Brom's first ever full time manager, he then managed Reading before moving to Weymouth where he ran a pub and then a hotel before his death aged 63 in June 1975.

## SMITH, Bobby

*Appearances:74 Goals:23 (1950-1955)*
*Career: Chelsea, Tottenham, Brighton (1950-1964).* A barnstorming centre forward, Smith was signed by manager Billy Birrell after being spotted in a junior match in Redcar, as a 15 year-old. He progressed on schoolboy forms through the juniors, intermediates, reserves and then into the first team, scoring goals all the way. He made his league debut as a 17 year-old against Bolton Wanderers in September 1950 and despite scoring 16 goals in 39 games the next season he lost his place to Roy Bentley and dropped back into the reserves almost until his sale midway through the 1955 Championship winning season. He was sold to Tottenham Hotspur who were seeking a replacement for Eddie Baily for bargain £18,000. Went onto win the double with Spurs. Became a painter & decorator and now lives in retirement in North London after suffering from ill health.

## SORRELL, Dennis

*Appearances: 4 Goals:1 (1962-1964)*
*Career: Leyton Orient, Chelsea, Leyton Orient. (1957-1966).* Signed from Leyton Orient for £10,000 in March 1962, making his debut in a home clash against Birmingham City as soon as he arrived at the club. From then on, found first team chances few and far between with Terry Venables and Ron Harris establishing themselves in the first team at the time. Scored his only goal in the FA Cup Fifth Round defeat against Manchester United in March 1963 and returned to Brisbane Road for £3,000 in September 1964. Ran a number of pubs and clubs in London's East End for 25 years before retiring.

## SPACKMAN, Nigel

*Appearances:179 Goals:14 (1983-1987 and 1992-1996)* . Career: *Bournemouth, Chelsea, Liverpool, QPR, Chelsea, Sheffield United. (1980-1996).* Signed in June 1983 for a bargain £40,000 as part of John Neal's rebuilding plans. He only missed two games all season as the Blues marched to the Division Two title in his first season. Then two years later, the lively midfielder was part of the Full Members Cup victory at Wembley before John Hollins sold him for ten times the sum that the club had originally paid out. Returned to the Bridge five years later for £485,000 a more mature player, but six games into his second spell he suffered a serious back injury which threatened his career. He was eventually released on a free transfer aged 35. Became assistant manager of Sheffield United and managed Barnsley before becoming a Sky pundit. Returned to management at Millwall, but has been a senior coach at the Glenn Hoddle Academy in Spain since 2008.

## SPARROW, John

*Appearances:74 Goals:2 (1974-1981)* Career: *Chelsea, Millwall, Exeter City. (1974-1983).* Made his debut as a 16 year-old in March 1974 and it appeared that the club finally had a natural successor to Eddie McCreadie. Sadly, he never quite fulfiled that expectation during seven seasons at the club and was sold to Exeter City for £10,000 in January 1981. Now owns a newsagents on Plymouth's Union Street.

## SPECTOR, Miles

*Appearances: 6 Goals:0 (1952-1953)* Career: *Chelsea, Millwall (1952-1956).* An amateur outside left who made his debut against Sunderland in February 1952 in place of Billy Gray and made an immediate impact. Also played in the epic FA Cup tie against WBA but was unable to hold down a regular place. Worked as an aircraft engineer for many years before going into teaching at Hendon Technical College. Now lives in retirement in Cornwall.

Photo: Danielle Shank (shankit4chesney)

## SPEEDIE, David

*Appearances:205 Goals:64 (1982-1987)*
Career: *Barnsley, Darlington, Chelsea, Coventry City, Liverpool, Blackburn Rovers, Southampton, Birmingham City, WBA, West Ham United, Leicester City. (1978-1995).* A brilliant but aggressive former coal miner, Speedie arrived at the club from Darlington in May1982 for £70,000 as a virtual unknown. He soon formed a fantastic partnership with Kerry Dixon with the main supply line coming from Pat Nevin. He was a pivotal member of the 1984 Second Division winning squad, chipping in 13 goals. Two years later, he netted a hat trick in the Full Members Cup Final victory over Manchester City. He stayed at the club for one more season and with the club in turmoil he was sold in to Coventry City for £750,000. Has worked as a football agent, is a partner in a recruitment company in Wigan but based in Dublin. Also has homes in Doncaster and Spain

## SPENCE, Dick

*Appearances:246 Goals:65 ((1934-1950))*
Career: *Barnsley, Chelsea. (1925-1950).* A nimble winger who arrived from Barnsley for £5,000 in October 1934. The 19 goals that he scored in his debut season quickly made him a firm favourite with the Stamford Bridge crowd. His sixteen years service saw him become one of only two players to play for the club on either side of World War 2 when he served in the Met Police. He later recovered from a broken leg to become the oldest player ever to play for the club at 39 years and 57 days. The record still stands today! Stayed on at the club for two decades after hanging up his boots, working with the juniors and 'A' team and was a regular at games right until his death in March 1983 aged 74.

## SPENCER, John

*Appearances: 103 Goals: 36 (1992-1996)*
Career: *Chelsea, Queens Park Rangers, Everton, (1992-1999).* A Catholic who made the controversial decision to start his career at protestant Rangers before a £450,000 switch to West London. He spent four years at Stamford Bridge, enjoying what is widely recognised as the best spell of his career. Was sold for £2.5 million soon into Ruud Gullit's reign at the club. Ended his career in the States with Colorado Rapids and is now assistant coach at Houston Dynamo

## STANIC, Mario

*Appearances:80 Goals:10 (2000-2004)*
Career: *Chelsea. (2000-2004).* The former Bosnian refugee signed for Chelsea for £5.6million in July 2000 and by the time he had retired he had played in six countries. He suffered from his fair share of injuries but could never be accused of giving anything but his best when he was fit. A member of the 2000 Charity Shield winning side, he was forced to retire because of a serious knee injury at the age of 32.

Photo: Dan Davies

## STANLEY, Gary

Appearances:120 Goals:15 (1971-1979)
Career: Chelsea, Everton, Swansea City, Portsmouth, Bristol City. (1975-1988). Stanley came recommended to the club by former Stamford Bridge star Frank Upton and showed much promise in his younger years. His best season was the 1976-77 promotion winning campaign when he played 38 games but missed out on the run-in because Eddie McCreadie felt that the pressure was starting to affect him. Having missed almost all of the next season because of a groin injury, there was hope that he would be able to re-capture the style that made him such a hit when he first came into the side. However, things were never the same and as a result, he was allowed to leave for Everton for £300,000 to ease some financial pressure. Lives in the Portsmouth area, where he worked for a cable television company before becoming a sales rep for a company called Colorama Pharmaceuticals.

## STEFFEN, Willi

Appearances: 20 Goals: 0 (1946-1947)
Career: Chelsea. (1946-1947). A former fighter pilot who was sent to London to learn English and it turned out his tutor was to be the wife of the then Chelsea manager Billy Birrell. This led to a trial being arranged, which turned out to be a 4-0 win over Bournemouth. He was soon in the first team making his debut at left back against Derby County in the FA Cup. Ironically, his last game was also against the Rams when he was made captain for the day. He needed to return home to complete his national service. Played for Young Boys of Berne for over a decade after he returned to Switzerland. He was running the family business which distributed fruit and veg from near his home, a 19th century cottage in Utzenstorf near Berne, right up to until his death in May 2005 aged 80. His grand-daughter is named Chelsea.

## STEIN, Mark

Appearances: 63 Goals: 25 (1993-1998)
Career: Luton Town, Aldershot Town, Queens Park Rangers, Oxford United, Stoke City, Chelsea, Stoke City, Ipswich Town, Bournemouth, Luton Town, Dagenham and Redbridge. (1984-2003). Cost the Blues £1.6 million and enjoyed a dream first season at Stamford Bridge. After failing to score in his first seven games, he went onto set a then Premier League record for scoring in seven successive matches between December and February, as well as starting the 1994 FA Cup Final. Niggling injuries then started to set in, but he regained his form after returning from an ankle operation. The arrival of Mark Hughes co-insided with Stein's goal touching deserting him and he never reached the same heights again. He became physiotherapist at Barnet but was released from his contract in April 2010 having been in the post for three years.

## STEPNEY, Alex

*Appearances:1 Goals:0 (1966)*
Career: *Millwall, Chelsea, Manchester United. (1963-1977).* Stepney's stay at Stamford Bridge lasted just four months. He was signed from Millwall for £50,000 in the summer of 1966 but was on his way to Old Trafford in the September, at a £5,000 profit, when Sir Matt Busy needed to replace Dave Gaskell and Harry Gregg. This was just ten days after making his one and only appearance against Southampton at the Dell. He ran a van hire business in Rochdale, also ran a pub, worked in a car body repair shop, became Commercial Manager at Rochdale FC and coached the goalkeepers at Man City. Is now an after dinner speaker and radio chat show host in Manchester.

## STRIDE, Dave

*Appearances:37 Goals:0 (1976-1980)*
Career: *Chelsea, Millwall, Leyton Orient. (1976-1985).* A left winger who was converted in a left back became one of the very few bright spots in the 1978-79 season after making his league debut against Derby County.

**Mark Stein**
*Photo: Ingy The Wingy*

The 20 year-old was to make the place in the side his own, embarking on a 33 game run in the team until a hairline fracture of the skull received in a game against Middlesbrough disrupted his progress. When the club needed to slash playing numbers, he was sold to Memphis Rangers for £90,000. Has coached local teams and is now working for a flooring company in his native Lymington

## STUART, Graham

*Appearances: 110 Goals: 18 (1989-1993)*
Career: *Chelsea, Everton, Sheffield United, Charlton Athletic, Norwich City. (1989-2005).* Scored on his home debut against Crystal Palace in April 1990 and then had to wait until the following November for his second game. Netted again against the Eagles at Stamford Bridge in his third first team appearance and became a regular in the first team. This helped him win England under-21 caps, but just as it seemed he had a bright future at the club under Glenn Hoddle, he decided to join Everton in 1993 on the eve of the new season for a tribunal settled fee of £850,000. Since retiring he has became a pundit with Sky Television and on radio, living on the North-West coast in Birkdale Village.

## STUBBS, Les

*Appearances: 123 Goals: 35 (1952-1958)*
Career: *Southend United, Chelsea, Southend United. (1948-1959).* A hard working, forceful inside left, Stubbs joined the club from his local club Southend in November 1952 for £10,000. He went on to score five goals in 27 games in the Blues 1955 Championship success under Ted Drake, one of which was the all important equaliser at Wolves. A key player for three years, he eventually returned to Roots Hall in 1957 with the Blues making a £2,000 profit and signing Alan Dicks as part of the deal. Lives on Great Wakering High Street and worked for the Fire Brigade.

## SUTTON, Chris

*Appearances: 39 Goals: 3 (1999-2000)*
Career: *Norwich City, Blackburn Rovers, Chelsea, Birmingham City, Aston Villa. (1991-2007).* When Chelsea lost Pierluigi Casiraghi, Mark Hughes and Gianluca Vialli in the summer of 1999, they broke the club record and paid £10million to bring Sutton to Stamford Bridge. The move was hardly a success after he took eight games to break his duck with a goal against Manchester United. Then after a 28 game run of firing blanks and with Jimmy Floyd Hasselbaink and Eidur Gudjohnsen the first choice striking partnership, he was sold to Celtic at a £4million loss. Has been manager of League Two Lincoln City since September 2009.

Photo: scott2342

## SWAIN, Kenny

*Appearances: 132 Goals: 29 (1973-1978)*
Career: *Wycombe Wanderers, Chelsea, Aston Villa, Nottingham Forest, Portsmouth, West Bromwich Albion, Crewe Alexandra. (1973-1994).* Was training to be a school teacher when he joined Chelsea from the amateur ranks at Wycombe Wanderers. Was given a chance on the left wing in 1974/75 as the club lurched towards relegation and was also deployed as a striker and a midfielder before once again being dropped in November 1978. This prompted him to ask for a move and was sold to raise cash, with Aston Villa paying £100,000 to take him to Villa Park. Managed Wigan and Grimsby Town, has scouted for clubs, was director of football at a private school and is now an FA coach working with the under-16's and under-17's

## TAMBLING, Bobby

*Appearances: 370 Goals: 202 (1958-1970)* Career: *Chelsea, Crystal Palace. (1958-1973).* One of the most prolific marksman in history with a record to rank among the very best. His total of 164 league goals is still a club-record. He got the ball rolling as a 17 year-old on his league debut. One of an elite band of players to score five goals in a game, he also netted four in a game four times. Became a promotion winner in 1963 and then scored in both the 1965 League Cup Final and the 1967 FA Cup Final defeat. Suffered from injuries towards the end of his Blues career. When he was fit again, Ian Hutchinson and Peter Osgood had become the first choice partnership and he was sold to Crystal Palace for £40,000 plus to Alan Birchenall. A Jehovah's Witness for many years, he ran a sports shop in Havant, Hampshire but in 1994 was declared bankrupt in the County court at Portsmouth. He had been working as a hod carrier but then moved to the Republic of Ireland, where he was involved in the building trade.

**GUESS WHO? - see page 150 for answers.** *Photo: Dan Davies*

Photo: www.unitednights.co.uk

## THOMAS, Mickey

*Appearances: 54  Goals: 11 (1984-1985)*
Career: Wrexham, Manchester United,
Everton, Brighton, Stoke City, Chelsea,
West Bromwich Albion, Derby County,
Shrewsbury Town, Leeds United, Stoke
City, Wrexham. (1971-1991). 'Tricky
Mickey' was a hard working midfielder
who had been in the game for a 13 years
by the time he was signed by John Neal,
the man who gave him his debut at
Wrexham, in a £75,000 deal in January
1984. He marked his first game with two
goals against leaders Sheffield
Wednesday and his contribution proved
vital in the march in the Second Division
title. Thomas never seemed to properly
settle at the club, driving back and forth to
his home in North Wales. He often slept in
the dressing rooms at the club training
ground and stayed in a homeless hostel.
Was eventually sold to WBA for £100,000
after new boss John Hollins signed Jerry
Murphy and Mickey Hazard. Became
youth coach at Wrexham until sentenced
for his part in a counterfeit money scam, is
now a radio summariser and an after
dinner speaker.

## THOMPSON, James W

*Appearances: 42  Goals: 34 (1927-1929)*
Career: Charlton Athletic, Wimbledon,
Millwall, Coventry, Leyton Orient,
Chelsea, Norwich City, Sunderland,
Fulham, Hull City. (1919-1932). A left
winger who was converted into a centre
forward with impressive results. Bagged
25 goals in 30 games in his first season,
only to find himself dropped at the start of
his second season following the signing of
Syd Elliott from Fulham. When he did get
a run of games, he found the net nine
times in 12 games. This was apparently
not enough to secure a starting place and
when he didn't get his position back he
departed for Norwich City, in May 1929.
Was manager of Dartford for a season
before returning to Stamford Bridge as a
scout. This proved to be his forte and he
went on to become a leading talent
spotter who was narrowly beaten to
signing a young Duncan Edwards. He
later discovered future stars Jimmy
Greaves, Terry Venables and Bobby
Tambling. Ended his career scouting for
Southampton and died in Epsom in
August 1984 aged 86.

## THOMSON, Charlie (Chic)

*Appearances: 59  Goals: 0 (1952-1957)*
Career: Chelsea, Nottingham Forest.
(1952-1961). The Scottish goalkeeper was
spotted playing for the army team during
his national service by Ted Drake, who
brought him to Chelsea from Clyde in
1952 for £5,000. He shared goalkeeping
duties with Bill Robertson and played 16
games in the 1955 Championship winning
season. By the time he left Stamford
Bridge for Nottingham Forest, with whom
he won an FA Cup winners' medal in
1959, he had kept 16 clean sheets in 59
appearances. He hung up his boots (and
gloves) in 1961 and lived in Nottingham
until his death in February 2009 aged 78.
He had worked as a social worker in the
area until his retirement.

## THOMSON, Jim

*Appearances: 47 Goals: 1 (1965-1968)*
Career: *Chelsea, Burnley (1965-1981).*
Was one of a number of young Scottish
players brought to the club by Tommy
Docherty but became a victim of his own
versatility, playing in seven different
positions during his time in the first team.
He enjoyed his best run in 1966-67 after
John Hollins asked for a transfer, making
29 of his 47 appearances. The arrival of
Dave Sexton soon afterwards was the
beginning of the end, as chances were
fewer and further between and a £40,000
move to Burnley in September 1968 was
the end result. He became a rep with a
brewery then Commercial Manager of
Burnley FC before working as a Sales
Director with Ben Shaw's Soft Drinks
Company in Huddersfield until returning
to the brewery business. He still lives in
Burnley.

## THOMSON, Robert

*Appearances: 95 Goals: 29 (1911-1922)*
Career: *Chelsea, Charlton Athletic. (1911-
1925).* A centre forward who lost his left
eye in a childhood firework accident, he
once scored seven goals in a London
Combination game against Luton Town.
He cost the club £200 from a non league
side and enjoyed a decent scoring record.
was named in the 1915 FA Cup losing
side after Vivian Woodward turned down a
chance play because he had been away
on military service. Thomson left after
World War One making the club a £100
profit. After hanging up his boots he
worked as a local government clerical
officer. He died in Croydon in
January1971 aged 81.

## TIAGO

*Appearances: 34 Goals: 4 (2004-2005)*
Career: *Braga, Benfica, Chelsea, Lyon,
Juventus, Atletico Madrid (loan) (1999-
2010).* Portuguese midfielder, signed for
Juventus from Lyon for £11 million in 2007
but spent the latter part of the 2009/10
season on loan to Atletico Madrid.

## TICKRIDGE, Sid

*Appearances: 73 Goals: 0 (1951-1955)*
Career: *Tottenham Hotspur, Chelsea,
Brentford. (1939-1957).* Moved to
Stamford Bridge for £10,000 in March
1951 after losing his place in the Spurs
team to Alf Ramsey. He proved to be a
more than useful signing, providing
stability to an otherwise suspect defence.
In four years at the Bridge, he played over
70 games before ending his career as a
player in west London with Brentford. His
entire football career had been spent in
the capital and this trend continued with a
spell as assistant trainer at Millwall, before
returning to White Hart Lane as trainer to
the youth team. It was here that he earned
a reputation for being very effective in
bringing on young players. Died in 1997

**Tiago**
*Photo: lucam*

**Ron Tindall in Australia.**

## TINDALL, Ron

*Appearances: 174 Goals: 70 (1953-1961)*
Career: *Chelsea, West Ham United, Reading, Portsmouth (1953-1969).* Spotted by Ted Drake and worked in the club offices before turning professional. An expert at flicking the ball on, he was useful in the air, with two thirds of his goals coming from headers. Scored on his debut against West Bromwich Albion and created plenty of chances for others, especially his striker partner Jimmy Greaves. Left to join West Ham after four years, in a £12,000 part exchange deal involving Andy Malcolm. An all rounder who also played cricket for Surrey, he scored over 5,000 runs and once missed the start of the soccer season because his side was chasing the county championship title. Also played for Reading and Portsmouth. Later also had spell as general manager and caretaker manager at Fratton Park. Was secretary of Waterlooville Golf Club before he emigrated to Perth, Australia, where he became state director of sport for Western Australia.

## TOOMER, Walter

*Appearances: 1 Goals: 0 (1905)*
Career: *Fulham, Chelsea, Southampton. (1905-1914).* An amateur throughout his career, he was a studying to be a teacher when he made his only appearance for Blues in their 7-1 FA Cup defeat to Crystal Palace in November 1905. Served in the Royal Artillery in France during the First World War, then became a schoolmaster in Southampton until taking over the running of his father's sports shop in the city. He was also a Southampton director. Died in December 1962 aged 79.

## TOWNROW, John

*Appearances: 140 Goals3: (1927-1932)*
Career: *Clapton Orient, Chelsea, Bristol Rovers. (1919-1932).* A capable centre half who was hit by more than his fair share of injuries during his stay at the club. Cool under pressure, he played 14 games in the 1929-30 promotion winning side, helping them establish themselves in the top flight the season afterwards. In total, he gave five years good service to the club. Was a coach and groundsman at Fairburn House and worked for Becton Gasworks, then for a brewer. Died in Knaresborough, Yorkshire in 1969 aged 68.

## TOWNSEND, Andy

*Appearances: 138 Goals: (1990-1993)*
Career: *Southampton, Norwich City, Chelsea, Aston Villa, Middlesbrough, WBA. (1985-2000).* A hard working midfielder who signed for £1.2million after Italia 90. He was capable of dominating anybody on his day and after a quiet start, started to show his influence and was voted Player of the Season. Took over as captain from Peter Nicholas and served the club well until he grew unsettled. Despite Glenn Hoddle's best efforts, he was sold to Aston Villa for £2.1 million. Became reserve team coach at WBA until leaving for a full time role in television with ITV, he also writes for the Daily Mail.

## TURNBULL, James

*Appearances: 22  Goals: 8 (1912-1914)*
Career: *Preston North End, Manchester United, Bradford Park Avenue, Chelsea. (1905-1914).* An aggressive inside/centre forward, Turnbull signed for £300 and went onto play an influential role in helping the club avoid relegation. Later went into business in the Chorlton area of Manchester where he ran a highly prosperous money lending business,. He died in the city in 1945.

## UPTON, Frank

*Appearances: 86  Goals: 3 (1961-1965)*
Career: *Northampton Town, Derby County, Chelsea, Derby County, Notts County (1953-1967).* A hard tackling, strongly built wing half known as 'Tank' played a vital role in the 1962-63 promotion winning season. He then helped The Blues establish themselves in the top flight before returning to Derby  in September 1965. Became player-manager of Workington, returned to the Bridge as assistant manager/coach and then became caretaker manager. A whole host of coaching jobs around the world followed and his last job was as Aston Villa's chief scout.  Opened a sports injuries clinic in Derby before retiring.

## VENABLES, Terry

*Appearances: 237  Goals: 31 (1960-1966)*
Career: *Chelsea, Tottenham, QPR, C. Palace, (1959-1974).* The hub of a well oiled machine, was an FA Cup winner in 1961 before playing a key role in the successful drive for promotion two years later. After forming a right flank axis with Ken Shellito and Bert Murray, he then captained League Cup winning side at Wembley in 1965. Always had an uneasy relationship with Tommy Docherty and was stripped of the captaincy soon after the Blackpool incident. He was placed on the transfer but the clubs directors insisted he stayed while they were still in the hunt for honours. Was eventually sold to Spurs for £80,000. A former England boss, Venables is one of the most colourful characters in the game, earned his nick name 'El Tel' in Barcelona and lost an expensive legal battle with Lord Sugar after a spell in charge of Spurs. Has also managed Australia, Crystal Palace, Middlesbrough, Leeds and was chairman of Portsmouth. Ran a drinking club Scribes in West London, co-created the television series Hazel and is still in much demand as a television and newspaper pundit.

*Photo: Thanks to Claire McConville*

Photo: Hannah Lee

## VERON, Juan Sebastian

*Appearances: 14 Goals: 1 (2003-2007)*
Career: *Manchester United, Chelsea. (2001-2007).* Hailed as one of the best midfielders in the world by Claudio Ranieri when he arrived from Manchester United for £15million Undoubtedly talented, but was shipped out to Inter Milan for two seasons loan by Jose Mourinho as soon as he arrived. He then went to Estudianates for the last year of his contract and has been playing for them ever since. Was part of Argentina's 2010 World Cup squad.

## VIALLI, Gianluca

*Appearances: 77 Goals: 40 (1996-1999)*
Career: *Chelsea (1996-1999).* A striker who just knew where the goal was every time he received the ball. One of a handful of players to have won all three of major three European club competitions, he also won the FA Cup in his first season at the club and went onto succeed Ruud Gullit as player manager. Won the Coca Cola Cup and Cup Winners Cup in his first season in charge and ended up winning five trophies in total before being sacked after spending £57 million on new players during his two and a half years in charge of first team affairs. Managed Watford but only lasted a season, is now working a commentator for Sky Italia.

Photo: Thanks to Christine Matthews

## VILJEON, Colin

*Appearances: 23  Goals: (1980-1982)*
Career: *Ipswich Town, Manchester City, Chelsea (1966-1982).* A South African born midfielder who became a British citizen in 1971. Was signed for £60,000 in March 1980 by Geoff Hurst when he was trying to get the club promoted from Division Two. He was never considered to be a first team regular but when John Neal took over as manager, he was recalled. An injury finally ended his chances and his contract was cancelled in May 1982. He became the licensee of a pub near Heathrow Airport when he hung up his boots but has since returned to South Africa to live in his home city Johannesburg, where he runs a coaching set up.

## WALDRON, Colin

*Appearances: 10  Goals: 0 (1967)*
Career: *Bury, Chelsea, Burnley, Manchester United, Sunderland, Rochdale. (1966-1979).* A very capable central defender who was signed for £30,000 from Bury in June 1967. He failed to settle in London and only played ten games before he was on his way back up north. He joined Burnley for what Chelsea paid in October 1967. Now runs Waldron Racing in Nelson, Lancashire. Also had business interests with Colin Bell in Bury.

## WALKER, Clive

*Appearances: 224  Goals: 65 (1975-1984)*
Career: *Chelsea, Sunderland, QPR, Fulham, Brighton, (1976-1993).* Hit the headlines when he scored two goals on his debut against Wolves at Molineux. He soon became a huge fans favourite, a fast winger who had the knack of scoring stunning goals. Enjoyed his best season in 1981-1982 when he netted 17 times, then in the next season with the club looking set to be relegated to Division Three he scored the winner at Bolton Wanderers to maintain their status. The emergence of Pat Nevin and a contract dispute saw him sold to Sunderland for £75,000. He returned to haunt the Blues when he denied them a place in the Milk Cup Final. Worked an auction House in Surrey, also ran a company with Jason Cundy. Is now an analyst for BBC Radio London and appears on Chelsea TV.

## WARREN, Benjamin

*Appearances: 101  Goals: 5 (1908-1912)*
Career: *Derby County, Chelsea. (1899-1912).* An England international who was recognised as being the best wing half and one of the most famous players in the country in his day. He couldn't help the club avoid relegation in the 1909-10 season and had to retire through ill health a couple of seasons later. Certified as being insane and spent time in a Derbyshire lunatic asylum before dying in tragic circumstances in Mickleover, Derbyshire aged just 37.

*Photo: Rod George*

## WATSON, Ian

*Appearances: 9 Goals: 1 (1960-1965)*
Career: *Chelsea, Queens Park Rangers.
(1960-1974).* A well built full back was
discovered by former Chelsea player Wilf
Chitty, he mainly spent his five seasons at
the club in the reserves. Had limited
chances in the first team, making his
debut in an FA Cup third round tie with
Tranmere Rovers and was allowed to move
to QPR in July 1965 for £10,000. Is now
retired living in Haywards Heath, Sussex.
He worked as a builder but now spends a
lot of his spare time playing for Lindfield
Bowling Club.

*Photo: United Nations Photo*

## WEAH, George

*Appearances: 15 Goals: 5 (2000)*
Career: *Chelsea , Manchester City.
(2000).* Won the FIFA World Player of the
Year, European Footballer of the Year and
African Footballer of the Year titles before
choosing to join the Blues on loan from AC
Milan ahead of AS Roma and Olympique
Marseilles. Scored the winner on his
debut against Tottenham after sitting
around the training ground all day waiting
for the club to get international clearance.
He also played a starring role in the
successful FA Cup campaign that season.
Is now back in his native Liberia where he
is a pursuing a career in politics.

## WEAVER, Sam

*Appearances: 125 Goals: 4 (1936-1945)*
Career: *Hull City, Newcastle United,
Chelsea, Stockport County. (1928-1947).*
A long throw specialist of his time, Weaver
quickly became a popular player in the
last few seasons before the World War
Two. Following his his £4,166 move from
Newcastle United in 1936, he was an
automatic choice at left wing half for the
last three seasons before war was
declared, and was appointed captain for
the 1938-39 season. The club had good
service out of him, but he had a lot more
to give. Played county cricket for
Somerset and was masseur to Derbyshire
CCC for many years. He also had jobs at
Leeds United and Millwall before going to
Mansfield as coach in September 1955.
He managed the Field Mill club, then
became assistant trainer and chief scout
before retiring in October 1980. Died in
Basford, Notts five years later aged 76.

## WEBB, David

*Appearances: 299 Goals: 33 (1968-1974)*
Career: *Leyton Orient, Southampton,
Chelsea, QPR, Leicester City, QPR,
Leicester City, Derby C, Bournemouth,
Torquay United. (1964-1984).* Few players
have been more popular at Stamford
Bridge than the cornerstone of Dave
Sexton's team. Twice voted Player of the
Year, in 1969 and 1972, he wore every
shirt possible except for the number 11,
even playing one game in goal against
Ipswich Town (and kept a clean sheet).
Bundled in Ian Hutchinson's long throw to
win the 1970 FA Cup Final replay against
Leeds and was a member of their winning
Cup Winners' Cup side 12 months later.
Was sold in July 1974 after six years at the
club for £100,000 when he grew unsettled
following the departures of Alan Hudson
and Peter Osgood. He did return as
manager between February and May
1993. Went on to manage Torquay,
Bournemouth, Southend, Yeovil and
Brentford. Lives in the New Forest and
Portugal and has property interests.

## WEGERLE, Roy

*Appearances: 28  Goals: 4 (1986-1988)*
Career: *Chelsea, Swindon Town, Luton Town, Queens Park Rangers, Blackburn Rovers, Coventry City. (1986-1995).* Born in South Africa, he never played football until university, when he was coached by former Ipswich Town goalkeeper Roy Bailey. Had a trial at Manchester United but went on to learn his trade in the NASL in America. Joined Chelsea in 1986 and despite being able to play on the wing or in the midfield, found chances hard to come by and Bobby Campbell sold him to Luton Town for £75,000. Is now a Pro golfer, playing the minor league gold tour and is also working for ESPN as a co-host of MLS Extratime. Lives in Palm Beach Gardens

## WELLER, Keith

*Appearances: 54  Goals: 15 (1970-1971)*
Career: *Tottenham Hotspur, Millwall, Chelsea, Leicester City. (1964-1978).* A midfielder who Dave Sexton wanted to convert into a goal scoring right winger when he arrived at the club in a £100,000 deal from Millwall. At first it appeared to be working a treat, when he scored 12 goals in his first half a season, but then the goals dried up. He managed to pick up a Cup Winners' Cup winner's medal in 1971, but was sold after just 16 months following the arrival of Chris Garland and

Steve Kember. Spent the next eight years at Leicester City, becoming one of their all time 'greats' and winning four England caps along the way. Ended his playing career in the States and went on to manage a number of clubs in Fort Lauderdale, Dallas, Houston and San Diego. Finally settled in Seattle where he drove an outside broadcast lorry for an American TV station before owning a coffee shop. He died in November 2004 after a long battle against cancer.

## WEST, Colin

*Appearances: 16  Goals: 4 (1985-1990)*
Career: *Chelsea, Swansea City, Hartlepool United. (1985-1994).* An England youth international striker who was quick, strong and aggressive. Was sent to Scottish outfit Patrick Thistle to gain first team experience and within days of returning he scored on his Chelsea debut in a League Cup tie against Arsenal. Then found chances few and far between, becoming surplus to requirements and was sold to Dundee in July 1990 for £105,000. Is back in his native Middlesbrough working as manager of the Stages Academy Homeless project after being a support manager for the English Churches Housing Group.

## WHIFFEN, Kingsley

*Appearances: 1  Goals: 0 (1967)*
Career: *Chelsea, Plymouth Argyle. (1967).* An apprentice who was only registered for one game in May 1967 when he stood in for Peter Bonetti who was rested for the match against Leicester, two weeks before the FA Cup Final. He also travelled to the States with Chelsea when Bonetti was away on international duty. Kingsley lived in Weymouth where he worked as a car salesman before helping out at his wife's hair salon until his death in December 2008. A keen golfer his family have donated the Kingsley Whiffen Memorial Cup to the Dorset County Golf Union county under-16 champion.

## WHITTAKER, Dick

*Appearances: 51 Goals: 0 (1952-1961)
Career: Chelsea, Peterborough United,
QPR. (1952-1961).* A Dublin born full back
who spent eleven years at Stamford
Bridge but he wasn't ever really seen as
anything other than a competent reserve.
Was mainly used as a deputy for one of
the Sillett brothers and enjoyed his best
season in 1958-59, when he played
eighteen games and was capped once by
his country. Later turned out for
Peterborough and QPR. Returned to the
Peterborough area in 1961, where he ran
a pub until he passed away September
1998 aged 64.

## WHITTON, William

*Appearances: 39 Goals: 19 (1923-1926)
Career: Chelsea. (1923-1926).* Failed to
make the grade at Spurs and was brought
to west London in a bid to end a goal
famine during an era when they were hard
to come by. He enjoyed his best season in
ironically what was to be his last
campaign, scoring 16 goals in 23 games
before having his contract cancelled in
April 1926. In spite of his creditable goal
scoring ratio, he decided to quit the game
to embark on a business career. Died in
Aldershot in April 1971.

## WICKS, Stan

*Appearances: 81 Goals: 1 (1954-1956)
Career: Reading, Chelsea. (1948-1956).* A
close friend of Roy Bentley, he followed
manager Ted Drake from his native
Reading to West London in a deal worth
£13,000. This turned out to be some of the
best money that the manager was to
spend during his tenure. A commanding
centre half, he shared duties with Ron
Greenwood during the 1955 title winning
season. Was stuck down by a knee injury
the following year, at the height of his
career and had to retire aged just 28. He
went into the family carpet business, but
died of cancer in 1983, aged 55.

## WICKS, Steve

*Appearances: 162 Goals: 8 (1974-1977 &
1986-1988) Career: Chelsea, Derby
County, Queens Park Rangers, Crystal
Palace, Queens Park Rangers, Chelsea.
(1974-1988).* A powerful centre half, who
just like his namesake Stan, hailed from
Reading. Became a first team regular at
the age of 19, partnering David Hay in
place of John Dempsey and Mickey Droy.
A member of the 1976-1977 promotion
winning team, he left for Derby County
shortly after the victory. He then returned
to Stamford Bridge seven years later for a
record £470,000 fee, but after three
games, John Hollins reverted to the Joe
McLaughlin/ Colin Pates partnership. He
attempted to battle back from a serious
back injury and was on the verge of a
move to Spurs, when he announced his
retirement and received £262,000
compensation. Had a spell as assistant
manager of Portsmouth, then went onto
manage Scarborough and Lincoln City,
had lucrative spells in Malaysia and
Singapore. Became a player's agent but
now works in corporate hospitality at
Queens Park Rangers' Loftus Road and
has invested in property.

## WILDING, Harry

*Appearances: 265 Goals: 25 (1914-1928)
Career: Chelsea, Tottenham Hotspur,
Bristol Rovers. (1914-1930).* Made a
scoring league debut as a centre forward
against Everton in August 1919 aged 25
and in total he spent fourteen and a half
seasons at Stamford Bridge. He moved
back to take on the role of centre half and
was a pillar of the side in the immediate
years after the war but then had to settle
for being in and out of the team. Was a
member of the London Victory Cup win
over Fulham, and contributed a goal to the
victory. Later moved to Tottenham before
returning to Chelsea, where he was
employed as groundsman. Died in
Earlsfield in December 1958 aged 64.

*Photo: Rod George*

## WILKINS, Graham

*Appearances: 149 Goals: 1 (1972-1982)*
*Career: Chelsea, Brentford, Southend
United. (1972-1984).* The eldest of four
footballing brother's, Graham was a full
back with good technique. Made his
debut as a 17 year-old against Ipswich on
Boxing Day 1972 but a broken leg at Old
Trafford a week later lost him nine months
of his footballing career. Competition from
Gary Locke then restricted his chances
but he plugged away. His effort was
rewarded when he became first choice
left back in Eddie McCreadie's 1976/77
promotion winning side until being
replaced by John Sparrow in the closing
weeks of the season. The arrival of Dennis
Rofe effectively ended his chances of a
regular place but he stayed at the club for
another two seasons before leaving for
Brentford. Was forced to quit after a
broken leg, then started to work for British
Airways at Heathrow Terminal Four, he
also buys and sells houses.

## WILKINS, Ray

*Appearances: 198 Goals:34 (1973-1979)*
*Career: Chelsea, Manchester United,
Queens Park Rangers, Crystal Palace,
Queens Park Rangers, Wycombe
Wanderers, Hibernian, Millwall, Leyton
Orient (1973-1997).* A glorious career
began at Chelsea, with a debut in 1973 at
the age of 17. A midfield playmaker with
superb passing ability, he was made the
club's youngest ever captain just 12
months later. He led the Blues to
promotion to the First Division, earning
himself the first of his back to back Player
of the Year awards, the second coming
after he returned from a groin injury to
guide the club to safety. In the 1978/79
season, he stopped enjoying his football
and was relieved of the captaincy by
Danny Blanchflower. When the club were
relegated, he rejoined former boss Dave
Sexton at Manchester United in a
£825,000 deal. Has managed QPR and
Fulham, held various other coaching and
management jobs and is currently the
club's assistant manager. Also provided
the voice over for Tango adverts in the
1990's and worked for Sky television as a
pundit for a number of years.

*Photo: illarterate*

## WILLEMSE, Stan

*Appearances: 221 Goals: 2 (1949-1956)*
*Career: Brighton & Hove Albion. Chelsea,*
*Leyton Orient. (1946-1958).* Having
served in the Royal Marines during the
second world war, he joined Chelsea from
Brighton for £6,500 in 1949. The transfer
fee apparently enabled the south coast
club to refurbish the South Stand at the
Goldstone Ground. He replaced Welsh
international Billy Hughes, becoming a
huge fans' favourite after establishing
himself as a regular in the team from 1952
onwards. Willemse only missed six games
in the 1955 title winning season,
partnering John Harris and then Peter
Sillett. It is reported that he raced home to
Brighton after the title victory to watch his
greyhounds run. Then, as the team broke
up he was sold to Leyton Orient for £4,500
in Jun 1956. After retiring he took over a
pub in Brighton before running a betting
shop in Southwick. He then became a
security officer at London University
before retiring to Hove, Sussex, where he
still lives.

## WILLIAMS, Paul

*Appearances: 1 Goals: 0 (1980-1983)*
*Career: Chelsea. (1980-1983).* A regular
at centre half for the youth and reserve
teams but couldn't make the big break
through. Played his only league game
standing in for Mickey Droy in a 2-2 draw
with Oldham Athletic in April 1983.

## WILLIAMS, William

*Appearances: 2 Goals: 0 (1927-1928)*
*Career: West Ham United, Chelsea.*
*(1922-1928).* Joined the club for one
season as deputy to Albert Thain. Stood in
for him in two games against Grimsby
Town and Reading in December 1927,
before being released to play non-league
football in Essex. He ran his own haulage
business before opening a tobacconist
and confectioners in Ilford where he died
in 1994 aged 89.

## WILSON, Andy

*Appearances: 253 Goals: 62 (1923-1931)*
*Career: Middlesbrough, Chelsea, Queens*
*Park Rangers. (1914-1932).* One of the
most popular and loyal players to have
worn the shirt in the years between the
two World Wars. He was certainly one of
the greatest players of the early 1920's, in
1923-1924 - was leading scorer for both
Middlesbrough and Chelsea, whom he
joined for £6,500 before making a goal
scoring debut against Preston. Wilson
was converted to an inside forward when
he moved to Stamford Bridge and spent
eight seasons at the club before moving to
QPR. He managed Walsall but never took
to the role, coached at Chelsea before
World War Two, after which he worked in
Westminster as a civil servant at the
Ministry of Works. He lived in London after
his retirement and was a regular at
Chelsea games. Died in October 1973
aged 77.

## WILSON, Clive

*Appearances: 103 Goals: 5 (1987-1990)*
*Career: Manchester City, Chester City,*
*Chelsea, Manchester City, Queens Park*
*Rangers, Tottenham Hotspur, Cambridge*
*United, (1979-2000).* Signed by The Blues
for £208,000 in March 1987 but stayed at
Maine Road to aid their fight against the
drop until the end of the season. Made his
belated debut against Sheffield Wednesday
in the following August. Played a large
part in the 1989 Division Two
championship winning season at left back
with Tony Dorigo but then was a bit part
player when he returned to midfield. He
won a Full Members Cup before leaving
for QPR months later for £450,000 in
search of regular first team football with
The Blues never really seeing him at his
best. Had a spell as a sales rep for Gilbert
Pollard Sports then had a job showing
prospective buyers around houses for
auction. In 2009 started he started
working at St John's CE Secondary
School, in Epping, Essex.

## WILSON, Kevin

*Appearances: 191 Goals: 55 (1987-1992)*
*Career: Derby County, Ipswich Town,*
*Chelsea, Notts County, Bradford City,*
*Walsall, Northampton Town. (1979-1997).*
A Northern Ireland international who
spent most of his first season at the club
on the sub's bench, but played an
influential role on both flanks in the club
winning the Division Two Championship in
1989. He was a member of the ZDS Cup
winning side a season later and was voted
Player of the Year. Fell out of favour with
Ian Porterfield who turned to Clive Allen
and was sold to Notts County on deadline
day in March 1992 for £225,000. Managed
Northampton as well as a number of non
league teams and has been in charge of
llkeston Town since 2009. Wilson, who is
also a consultant at FootballCV academy,
after starting out with them as Football
Manager, has also worked in teacher
training in Roehampton.

## WINTER, Danny

*Appearances: 155 Goals: 0 (1945-1951)*
*Career: Bolton Wanderers, Chelsea.*
*(1936-1951).* Was a guest for The Blues
during the Second World War, helping
them to victory in the 1945 Football
League Cup South Final at Wembley,
proved to be a bargain signing at £5,000.
Became a fixture in the side for the first
four post war seasons at right back and
was a committee member of the PFA
during his time at Stamford Bridge. An
ankle injury forced his retirement from the
full time game and he returned to south
Wales via Worcester City. He worked in
the family building business before taking
a job for British Airways. Died in Trealaw,
South Wales in March 2004 aged 86.

## WISE, Dennis

*Appearances: 445 Goals: 75 (1990-2001)*
*Career: Wimbledon, Chelsea, Leicester
City, Millwall, Southampton, Coventry
City. (1985-2006).* The combative
midfielder Is the Blues' second most
successful ever captain behind John Terry.
A controversial figure both on and off the
pitch, he cost Chelsea a then record fee of
£1.6 million, and was twice voted player of
the year. His eleven year Stamford Bridge
career ended in 2001 when Claudio
Ranieri decided that he wanted to lower
the age of the squad. A stormy spell at
Leicester ended when he was sacked for
breaking a team mate's jaw. Moved to
Millwall where he became player-
manager, leading the Lions to an FA Cup
Final appearance and into Europe. Went
onto manage Swindon and Leeds before
landing an executive role at Newcastle
United in January 2008 until April 2009.

## WOOD Darren

*Appearances: 176 Goals: 4 (1984-1989)*
*Career: Middlesbrough, Chelsea,
Sheffield Wednesday. (1981-1989).*
Signed by his former Boro boss John Neal
in September 1984 in a £50,000 deal plus
Tony McAndrew, with the view to playing
in midfield. Instead, he made the right
back birth his own proving to be a
valuable asset in the 1986 Full Members
Cup winning side. He was at the club for
the first half of the 1989 promotion
winning campaign before moving to
Sheffield Wednesday in a shock £450,000
transfer. An injury forced him to retire
after just a handful of appearances.
Returned to his home town Scarborough
where he helped his father in his fish
wholesale business then started his own
business supplying meat to delicatessen.

Photo: Mark Freeman

## WOODLEY, Victor

*Appearances: 272 Goals: 0 (1931-1946)*
Career: *Chelsea, Derby County. (1931-1946).* One of the clubs best ever goalkeepers, Woodley became a fixture in the Chelsea goal within a matter of weeks after his move from non league Windsor & Eton, despite competition from Scotland international Johnny Jackson. Lost the best years of his stay in the capital to World War Two, which also ended his England career. He helped Chelsea to the Football League South Cup Final success and his last match for the club was a friendly against Dynamo Moscow which attracted a 100,000 crowd to Stamford Bridge. Moved back to the West Country, became a licensee at Bradford-Upon-Avon where he lived until his death in 1978 aged 68.

## WOODWARD, Vivian

*Appearances: 116 Goals: 34 (1909-1915)*
Career: *Tottenham Hotspur, Chelsea. (1901-1915).* An expert dribbler, brilliant on the ground and seen as one of the greatest amateur marksman of all-time. He arrived at the club after his 30th birthday but missed out on the 1915 FA Cup Final. Despite being granted leave from the army to play in the game, he stood down at the last minute to allow Bob Thomson, who scored seven goals in the earlier rounds to play. Later acted as a director of Spurs and Chelsea. He was an architect for most of his working life, then became a gentleman-farmer in the 1940's. Died in an Ealing nursing home after a long illness aged 74 in February 1954,

## WOSAHLO, Roger

*Appearances: 1 Goals: 0 (1964-1967)*
Career: *Chelsea, Ipswich Town, Peterborough United, Ipswich Town. (1964-1970).* Leading scorer for the juniors during his time at Stamford Bridge but the only chance he got in the first team was as a substitute against Stoke City in April 1967 when senior players were rested ahead of the FA Cup Final. He was

denied a debut goal by Gordon Banks! He emigrated to South Africa in 1970 but returned three years later. Worked for Autoglass as an area manager for 10 years before starting his own business called Ipswich Car Glass and Trim. Is also football development manager at Ipswich Wanderers.

Photo: illarterate

## WRIGHT-PHILLIPS, Shaun

*Appearances: 82 Goals: 4 (2005-2008)*
Career: *Manchester City, Chelsea, Manchester City (1998-2010).* Returned to Manchester City, his first club, in August 2008.

## YOUNG, Allan

*Appearances: 26 Goals: 1 (1961-1969)*
Career: *Arsenal, Chelsea, Torquay United, Wimbledon. (1959-1971).* Signed for £6,000 as cover for Marvin Hinton but he found his chances very limited during his stay at the club. Made just 26 outings in seven seasons, and his only League Cup appearance was in the 1965 Final but he was dropped for the replay. Was sold to Torquay for £2,000 more than he was bought for. He went into the catering business, as well as working at both Arsenal and West Ham, he later ran a pub in Enfield before his death in December 2009 aged 68 in Cheshunt. He had been suffering from motor neurone disease.

*Photo: Feggy Art*

## ZENDEN, Boudewijn
*Appearances: 43  Goals: 4 (2001-2004)*
Career: *PSV, Barcelona, Chelsea, Middlesbrough, Liverpool, Marseille, Sunderland (1993-2010).* Zenden declared that he wanted to end his playing career in England having spent two years in France playing for Marseille. Accordingly, he signed for Sunderland in October 2009.

Photo: Mark Page

## ZOLA, Gianfranco
*Appearances: 312  Goals: 80 (1996-2003)*
Career: *Chelsea (1996-2003).* Arrived at Stamford Bridge for £4.5 million after the then Parma boss Carlo Ancelotti decided that he was a 'square peg'. Went on to become Chelsea's greatest ever player , and even though his number 25 shirt has never officially been retired no player has worn it since he left the club. He was a true artiste, he could shoot and dribble, and scored the winner in the Cup Winners Cup Final. 'Franco' won a whole host of accolade's before ending his career in Italy. Became assistant to the Italian under-21 team managed by his former Chelsea team mate Pierluigi Casiraghi. Was appointed West Ham boss in September 2008, until he was sacked in June 2010.

## ZORICICH, Chris
*Appearances: 0  Goals: 0 (1997)*
Career: *Leyton Orient, Chelsea. (1989-1997).* A New Zealand international defender who O's fans staged a protest outside the Home Office to keep in the country. He never played a first team game for the Blues but did feature for the reserves. Now runs Blue Car Services Professional Chauffeurs.

• • • • • • • • • • • • • • • • • • • • • • • • • • • • •

# THE MANAGERS

## David Calderhead
He arrived at Stamford Bridge in 1907, a year after leading Lincoln City to an FA Cup win over the club. He was Club's first full-time manager/secretary and his 26 years at the club is the longest running manager in Chelsea history. He led the club to promotion once and relegation twice, he was also in charge when they reached the 1915 FA Cup Final. His media shyness earned the nickname 'the Sphinx of Stamford Bridge'. Never afraid to splash out on big name strikers, he left the club in June 1933 but continued to live in retirement in London for five years until his death in January 1938 aged 73.

## Leslie Knighton
Already had experience of managing Huddersfield Town, Arsenal , Bournemouth and Birmingham City before he took over at Chelsea from the long serving Dave Calderhead. Despite this, was unable to bring the silverware to Stamford Bridge that the club craved and he had to battle relegation for much of the six years that he spent at the club. He left the coaching to others and was rarely seen by the players during the week. Knighton stood down to let a younger man come in and had spell in charge of Shrewsbury before moving back to Bournemouth. Suffered ill-health but worked as a golf club secretary. Died in May 1959 aged 72.

# Billy Birrell

Billy Birrell took over the club when the storm clouds of war were gathering over Europe. Chelsea had an aging squad, most of whom retired just before war broke out, so Birrell in keeping with the country at the time had to make do and mend for seven years, never knowing from week to week, the side that the club would be able to put out. Still managed two War Time Cup Final appearances and when peace time broke out he had to recruit a new side from scratch. He twice managed to steer the club into the semi finals of the FA Cup as well as avoiding relegation in 1951 when they won their last three games to stay up. He started the youth policy which was to serve the club well over the subsequent years and worked as an office clerk in Kenton, where his son was a solicitor. Died in November 1968 aged 71.

# Ted Drake

A fearless centre forward as a player and from the first day he took over at Stamford Bridge, he set about revolutionising a club that was stuck in the past. He ditched the pensioner from the club badge replacing it with a roaring Lion. this was followed quickly by the music hall image as he would swap his suit for a track suit. A great motivator, and by the end of his third season in the charge the club won their only League title in the 20th century. Sadly, things soon went downhill, with an aging squad and youngsters who couldn't fulfil early promise. After ten seasons he was dismissed to become a turf accountant and commercial salesman with a spell as Barcelona assistant manager in between. Returned to football as reserve team manager at Fulham and then worked as chief scout until his retirement in the mid-1980's. Drake was later president of Hampshire CCC whom he played county cricket. He died at his home in Raynes Park in May 1995 aged 82.

# Tommy Docherty

See player section

# Dave Sexton

Already a well known figure at the club after serving The Doc for three years as assistant coach, it was player power that persuaded the board to appoint him. The club finished runners up to Wolves in his first season in charge, then in 1970, victory over Leeds United secured the FA Cup. 12 months later Real Madrid were beaten to win the Cup Winners' Cup but the player power that saw him appointed, got him the sack despite the directors initially backing him and selling several star names. Then in October 1975, he was dismissed. Ironically, he then succeeded Docherty at Manchester United after a stint at QPR. He twice managed the England under-21 team either side of managing Coventry. He was the first Technical Director at the FA's National School at Lilleshall and now lives in retirement in Kenilworth, Warwickshire

# Ron Suart

Ron had already managed three clubs stretching back to Wigan Athletic in 1955 when he took over at Stamford Bridge. He had also spent seven seasons as Tommy Docherty's assistant and was briefly caretaker manager before Dave Sexton retained his services. He finally got his chance in the hot seat, even though he left much of the training ground work to Eddie McCreadie. Money was spent but they were unable to halt the slide into the Second Division and he was moved sideways to become general manager. Remained in this post until 1978 when he became chief coach, finally leaving in February 1983. He was appointed chief scout by Wimbledon until he was released in February 2002 aged 82.

# Eddie McCreadie

See players section

## Ken Shellito

See players section

## Danny Blanchflower

The Blues were desperate for an experienced head when they turned to the Spurs legend. He had just finished a stint as Northern Ireland manager and was working as a journalist for the Sunday Express but hadn't had any day to day involvement with a football club for 15 years. Despite this, he agreed to become the fifth manager in as many years. He took over a squad past its sell-by date and soon found himself struggling to turn things around. After only ten months in the hot seat it was decided that another manager was needed and Blanchflower returned to his job on Fleet Street until his retirement. He suffered from Alzheimer's disease and died at his London home in December 1993 aged 67.

## Sir Geoff Hurst

England's World Cup Final hat trick hero was working as Danny Blanchflower's assistant for four months and was the fourth successive incumbent into the Stamford Bridge hot seat with no league management experience, having previously only been in charge of Southern League Telford United. In his first season, the Blues were top of the table, but a disastrous Easter period only produced a single point and ended any hopes of promotion. A 33 man squad was trimmed and experience in the shape of Dennis Rofe and Colin Viljoen was signed. They were well placed behind West Ham in the promotion race but a catastrophic capitulation saw a dramatic collapse of their promotion chances and the board, which included Ken Bates, decided another change in management was needed. Hurst went onto become the director of a insurance company and these days he represents a number of blue chip companies.

## John Neal

Twelve years of management experience at Wrexham and Middlesbrough had prepared John Neal for the task that laid ahead of him at Stamford Bridge. He was the first experienced incoming manager for six years and he had the backing of new chairman, Ken Bates. For the first couple of seasons the club struggled and narrowly avoided relegation to the Third Division. It was enough to shock the club into action and several long serving stars were shipped out. The new look Chelsea swept all before them, winning the Second Division Championship. On their return to the top flight, secured fifth place and a League Cup semi final, which underlined how far the club had progressed. Neal departed the club in the summer of 1985. Although a shock at the time, he had undergone heart surgery 12 months earlier and had been grooming John Hollins for his job. He now lives in retirement in Edinburgh.

## John Hollins

See players section

## Bobby Campbell

Bobby arrived at Stamford Bridge with a long record in management having been in charge at Fulham and Portsmouth, assistant manager of Aldershot and coached at QPR, Arsenal and Fulham. Initially employed as a coach, he took over from John Hollins towards in the end of the 1987-88 season and his guiding hand saw the Second Division title bagged by 17 points. Only on their return to the top flight did he splash out almost £3.4m on new players. The spending continued but results didn't improve and his three year stint in charge of the club was ended in the closing weeks of the 1990-91 season. He became personal assistant to Ken Bates before coaching in Kuwait. Now retired, he is these days in Roman Abramovich's inner circle.

## Ian Porterfield

Not the first choice of chairman Ken Bates - approaches for two other lower division managers were rebuffed, but Porterfield was available after being sacked by Reading. He spent £6 million on new players during his spell in charge at the Bridge but with little success. It was therefore no surprise that he was sacked in February 1992. Despite this, he wasn't out of work for long and took over the Zambian national team shortly after 18 members of the team had died in plane crash. He also coached a Saudi Arabia and was assistant manager at Bolton Wanderers before taking in Zimbabwe, Trinidad and Tobago and Armenia. In July 1988 married Elaine Allister, the daughter of former Chelsea star Jack but they were later divorced. Porterfield died of colon cancer in September 2007.

## David Webb
## Glenn Hoddle
## Ruud Gullit
## Gianluca Vialli

See players section

## Claudio Ranieri

The Italian was the first Blues manager to see the benefit of Roman Abramovich's billions and also the first to be sacked when he failed to deliver. He has since managed Valencia, Parma, Juventus and since 2009, Roma.

**The 'Special One'** *Photo: apascutio*

## Jose Mourinho

The 'Special One' delivered the club their first title since Ted Drake but couldn't bring Abramovich the trophy he courted the most, the Champions League. Since leaving the Bridge, he has enjoyed success with Inter Milan and is now looking to turn Real Madrid back into silverware winning outfit.

*Photo: Whistling in the Dark*

## Avram Grant

The Israeli was unfortunate enough to oversee Portsmouth's drop from the Premier League and is now in charge at West Ham United.

## Luiz Felipe Scolari

Big Phil had a spell at Uzbekistani champions Bunyodkor but since June 2010 has been in charge of Palmeiras.

## Guus Hiddink

Combined managing the Blues with being in charge of the Russian national team. Is now the Turkish national coach.

# Acknowledgments

Many thanks must go to Leigh Edwards, Ronnie Pilowski of the Western Province Cricket Umpires Association, Michael Weeks, Cornwall Cricket Media Officer/ Webmaster, Andy Riddle the secretary of the former Plymouth Argyle Players Association, David Ballheimer, Neil Barnet, Mark Westward the manager of the Chelsea Old Boys, Chris & Jan Cornish, Christine Matthews, Lyn Osgood, Katharine Pringle.

# Bibliography

**Football Club the first 100 years**
Ballheimer, David and Lush, Peter Hendon
(London League Publications)
**Chelsea – Complete Record 1905-1991**
Cheshire, Scott. (Breedon Sports Books)
**The Legends of Chelsea**
Cheshire, Scott.(Breedon Books)
**Glorious Canaries**
**Norwich City Football Club**
Davage, Mike.

**Chelsea, Champions of England 1954-55**
Hadgraft, Rob. (Desert Island Books)
**The PFA Premier League and Football League Record 1949-1998**
Hugman, Barry J.
(Lennard Queen Anne Press)
**The Men who Made Leyton Orient Football Club**
Kaufman, Neilson N. (Tempus)
**An English Football Internationals Who's who**
Lamming, D. (Hutton Press)
**Chelsea Player by Player**
Lovering, Peter. (Hamlyn)
**Who's who of Chelsea**
Matthews, T. (Mainstream Publishing)
**Plymouth Argyle Thanks for the Memory**
Rhodes, Steve. (Stevrho Publishing)
**Breedon Book of Football Managers**
Turner, Dennis and White Alex.
(Breedon Sports Books)
**Where Are They Now?**
Pringle Andy, Fissler, Neil.
(Two Heads Publishing)
**Chelsea Here Chelsea There**
Worrell Mark, Barker Kelvin, Johnstone David. (Gate 17)

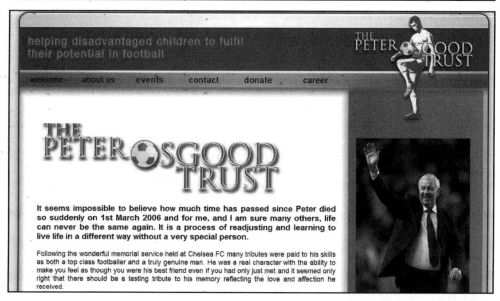

helping disadvantaged children to fulfil their potential in football

THE PETER OSGOOD TRUST

welcome    about us    events    contact    donate    career

It seems impossible to believe how much time has passed since Peter died so suddenly on 1st March 2006 and for me, and I am sure many others, life can never be the same again. It is a process of readjusting and learning to live life in a different way without a very special person.

Following the wonderful memorial service held at Chelsea FC many tributes were paid to his skills as both a top class footballer and a truly genuine man. He was a real character with the ability to make you feel as though you were his best friend even if you had only just met and it seemed only right that there should be a lasting tribute to his memory reflecting the love and affection he received.

The Peter Osgood Trust is a Charitable Organisation set up to help underprivileged children get a head start in life through sporting means. Please visit **www.thepeterosgoodtrust.org** to find out more - they would be extremely grateful for your support.

# Photographs

We are extremely grateful to the many photographers who have kindly allowed us to use their work.

Special thanks is due to....

**Associated Sports Photography**
(www.sports-photos.co.uk)
**Mirrorpix**
(www.mirrorpix.co.uk)
**Dan Davies**
(www.ddpix.co.uk)
**Rod George**
**Rowan Farnham-Long**

**apasciuto**
flickr.com/photos/apasciuto
**artefatte w**
flickr.com/photos/27116345@N05
**-AX-**
flickr.com/photos/axelrd
**Badger Swan**
flickr.com/photos/badgerswan
**Byron and Tamara**
flickr.com/photos/20492214@N00
**CamW**
en.wikipedia.org/wiki/User:Camw
**Claire McConville**
claires-rosleaancestry.co.uk
**Commander Idham**
flickr.com/photos/14104705@N08
**Comrad Fomin**
flickr.com/photos/andrei_fomin
**Crystian Cruz**
flickr.com/photos/crystiancruz
**Dan Avraham**
flickr.com/photos/33908615@N03
**Dennis Wareing**
flickr.com/photos/33929254@N07
**Dmason**
flickr.com/photos/dmason
**East Ham Bull**
flickr.com/photos/easthambull
**England 2018 Bid**
flickr.com/photos/england2018bid
**Feggy Art**
flickr.com/photos/28832703@N00
**Hannah Lee**
flickr.com/photos/iamhannah
**hanszinsli**
flickr.com/photos/11523338@N00
**Human Alien**
flickr.com/photos/24668475@N07
**ikoma**
flickr.com/photos/35034345570@N01

**illarterate**
flickr.com/photos/illarterate
**In The City 2009**
flickr.com/photos/inthecity2009
**Ingy The Wingy**
flickr.com/photos/ingythewingy
**ivan_siprak**
flickr.com/photos/yazoo07
**Jason Bagley**
flickr.com/photos/jbagley
**Joe Gazman**
flickr.com/photos/96961822@N00
**John Dobson**
flickr.com/photos/johnsworld
**jspace3**
flickr.com/photos/83895961@N00
**Kate Boydell**
flickr.com/photos/62719770@N00
**l3nnon1975 w**
flickr.com/photos/29408228@N07
**Lancs & Cheshire Amateur Football League**
landc.org.uk
**Louise Haigh**
flickr.com/photos/13422708@N08
**lucam w**
flickr.com/photos/59951793@N00
**Marathon Mitch**
flickr.com/photos/23020701@N05
**Mark Freeman (Free-ers)**
flickr.com/photos/46357488@N00
**Mark Page**
flickr.com/photos/7603426@N03
**Mattias Olsson**
flickr.com/photos/49503121126@N01
**Michael Kjaer**
flickr.com/photos/14933298@N0
**mpozzobon**
flickr.com/photos/mpozzobon
**Nick Sarebi**
flickr.com/photos/34517490@N00
**Rechigi Park Hotel**
flickr.com/photos/rechigiparkhotel
**Retro Reds**
retroreds.co.uk
**rowanfarnhamlong**
flickr.com/photos/36710290@N02
**sbstheworldgame**
flickr.com/photos/51387389@N0
**Scott2342**
flickr.com/photos/sjungling
**shankit4chesney**
flickr.com/photos/shankit4chesney
**Sicknote 10**
www.wikipedia.com
**Soccer C**
flickr.com/photos/soccerc
**SpreePix**
flickr.com/photos/44787195@N0
**Steffe**
flickr.com/photos/steffe

**Steindy**
commons.wikimedia.org/wiki/User:Steindy
**sueandandyj56**
flickr.com/photos/35674491@N08
**Sylvia Gutiérrez**
flickr.com/photos/50049999@N00
**Tapdown**
flickr.com/photos/28621656@N06
**terrygil999**
flickr.com/photos/terrygil999/
**The Prostate Cancer Charity**
flickr.com/photos/tppcuk
**toksuede**
flickr.com/photos/85348350@N00
**United Nations Photo**
flickr.com/photos/un_photo
**Wally Gobetz**
flickr.com/photos/wallyg
**Whistling in the Dark**
flickr.com/photos/yaffamedia
**William Bedzrah**
flickr.com/photos/13677626@N00
**wkocian**
flickr.com/photos/wkocjan

Every effort has been made tocontact copyright holders of photographs, where known, and they have been credited accordingly. We apologise to any copyright holder who we have not been able to contact.Where this is the case, plese contact us and we will rectify matters in future editions of this book.

# Guess Who?

Many former players give up their time to play for charitable causes and should be praised for doing so. Ex-Chelsea stars include...
P6.     Ian Britton
P11.    Kerry Dixon
P23.    Keith Dublin
P33.    Ray Wilkins
(sorry about the photo Ray!)
P36.    John Bumstead
P39.    Trevor Aylott
P43.    Ken Monkou
P49.    Tommy Langley
P 60.   Paul Canoville
P78.    Peter Bonetti
P84.    Graham Wilkins
P87.    Steve Finnieston
P99.    Clive Walker
P111.  Jason Cundy
P117.  Peter Rhodes-Brown
P128.  Gary Stanley